BANKS I.

BEAUFORT SEA

VICTORIA

70°N

ISLAND

TUKTOYAKTUK

ARCTIC CIRCLE

Great Bear Lake

YUKON
TERR.

DEMPSTER HIGHWAY

DAWSON
CITY

NORTHWEST

CANADA

Pelly Crossing

Wrigley

ARMACKS

TERRITORIES

WHITEHORSE

FRANCES LAKE

Great Slave Lake

TESLIN LAKE

WATSON LAKE

Skagway

Lower Post

INEAU

Fort Nelson

BRITISH

ALBERTA

Telegraph Creek

tka

COLUMBIA

Wrangell

Stewart

Peace River

Down North

Down North

PROFILES FROM ALASKA

AND THE YUKON

William L. Pohl

WITH PHOTOGRAPHS BY

Jock Conyngham

THORNDIKE PRESS
Thorndike, Maine

Library of Congress Cataloging-in-Publication Data

Pohl, William L., 1955-
    Down north.

    1. Yukon River Valley (Yukon and Alaska) — Social
life and customs.   2. Yukon River Valley (Yukon and
Alaska) — Biography.   3. Interviews — Yukon River Valley
(Yukon and Alaska)   I. Conyngham, Jock, 1956-
II. Title.
F912.Y9P64   1986   979.8′6   86-5741
ISBN 0-89621-086-3

Cover photographs by Jock Conyngham.

Cover design by Abby Trudeau.

Book design by Guy Fleming.

Book layout by Andrea Stark.

Typography by Camden Type 'n Graphics.

First Printing.

Contents

Introduction

JUST BEFORE MIDNIGHT ON THE DEMPSTER HIGHWAY, *the sun is faintly visible in the pewter gloaming. Soft light reflects on drizzle that blows across rolling tundra. This twilight will last until three in the morning when the sky begins to lighten again.*

Jock Conyngham and I left New York for Alaska in July 1979. Our route took us north to the trans-Canada highway and into the Yukon Territory in my car, a Buick Opel Manta built in '73. From Dawson Creek to the Alaska-Canada (Alcan) Highway, the car was coated with mud and oil, the latter slicked on the unpaved road to keep dust down. Gravel kicked up by semis cracked the windshield. Balljacks, jammed into the rear suspension coils, kept the car from bottoming in the ruts; the bug screen kept the radiator from clogging; and a rubber mat over the gas tank prevented disastrous leaks. Nothing, how-

ever, stopped a tiny field mouse from dying in the air vent.

The Dempster Highway is a 460-mile-long strip of dirt that slices through spruce forests and barren tundra from Klondyke Junction to Inuvik in the Northwest Territories. When the muskeg freezes, a four-wheel drive can continue to Tuktoyaktuk on the Bering Sea.

The highway was named for W. J. D. Dempster, a corporal in the Royal North West Mounted Police. In 1911 he located a lost patrol, led by Inspector Francis Fitzgerald, that had frozen to death in a blizzard. The highway loosely follows Dempster's dog sled route.

Although construction started on the Dempster in the late 1950s, the road was not yet officially open 20 years later. Nonetheless, this road to the Arctic Sea is a marvel of engineering, elevated on gravel berms that insulate its mud and shale from permafrost. A paved road would never survive the extremes of temperature.

There are no gas stations, apart from government highway maintenance camps, for 236 miles. Then one reaches the Eagle Plains Hotel, complete with satellite television. The hotel bar is named for Spike Millen, a Northwest Canadian mounted policeman killed by Albert Johnson, the "Mad Trapper of Rat River."

Johnson came into the territory from Fort McPherson in 1931. He built a cabin, set trap lines, and in the cold dark winter, he snapped. When he began to spring the lines of other trappers, a native named William Nerysoo complained. Spike Millen was dispatched to investigate.

When Millen was found dead with a bullet through his chest, the Mounties formed a posse and hunted Johnson down.

8

They dynamited the trapper from his cabin and a six-week chase through the Richardson Mountains followed.

Johnson's endurance was superhuman. On snowshoes he carried a 200-pound rucksack and three rifles through deep drifts. The posse didn't catch up with him until he was near Old Crow, 100 miles from his cabin.

Johnson was finally routed from the hills by an airplane flown by "Wop" May, a bush pilot credited in World War I with having narrowly escaped Manfred von Richthofen, the "Red Baron." The trapper made a last stand in the open, wounding three Mounties and killing one. Shot six times, he returned fire until a seventh slug severed his spine. The posse found Johnson's last meal in the rucksack—a frozen squirrel and some whiskey.

Post-mortem photographs of Johnson's partially decomposed face hang in the Spike Millen Lounge at the Hotel. Tourists from a Greyhound Scenicruiser, which had to be towed from the mud on its maiden trip up the highway, regard these photographs with morbid curiosity.

Jock and I passed through Eagle Plains and camped near the 66th parallel, marked by an oversized truck tire lynched by the road. A handwritten sign labeled it, "Arctic Circle." It was adorned with graffiti and dents from shotgun pellets.

The next morning, we woke to the breaking of a storm. It had been raining for two weeks, and thick fog rolled across nameless valleys. Stands of stunted spruce rose from banks of silty rivers. Even in summer, sculptured mounds of dirty snow lingered in the shade.

We reached Inuvik that afternoon. It is a collection of muddy streets, a Hudson's Bay Company store, and a hotel, all tied together by a utilidor—an above-ground network of pipes that carry steam to the buildings. The utilidor, like the sidewalks, is insulated with styrofoam. Many of the houses are perched on stilts to prevent meltdowns into the permafrost.

The local church serves God. The Mad Trapper Saloon serves everyone else—Dome Petroleum employees who work on offshore oil rigs, and the native Inuit for whom the town was originally built.

Dollar bills are posted on the rafters of the saloon. Traditionally, trappers signed the money. It was bush credit in hard times. Today, the money is signed by people in the oil business.

In the saloon we meet Bob McKenzie. He used money from furs he trapped on Herschel Island to buy a 50-foot privateer ketch which he named Ungaluk—the West Wind. *He sailed it from Rhode Island through the Panama Canal and up into the Beaufort Sea. He runs a charter business but agrees to take us, free of charge, down north on the MacKenzie River to Tuktoyaktuk. (Rivers in the arctic watershed flow "down" along the North Slope.)*

The first person to greet us at the docks several days later is an Inuit woman. On the front of her sweatshirt is the question: "Where the hell is Tuktoyaktuk?" On the back, "Who the hell cares?"

Tuk Tuk is a land of contrasts. A musk-ox hide is draped over a snowmobile. Dog sleds lie stacked in the backs of GMC pickups. Skin kayaks are moored by Cessna float planes. Caribou antlers are nailed over the doorways of native shanties in view of prefabricated Dome company dormitories. The town is home to beluga whale hunters and military personnel stationed at a Dis-

tant Early Warning line radar barracks.

When the fire station sounds its whistle, scores of sled dogs staked in backyards bay in eerie chorus, heads thrown back, eyes closed. The concert makes the grassy spit seem even more remote.

We hitched back to Inuvik with a pilot who worked for Ken Borek Airlines. What took 24 hours on the Ungaluk whizzed by in 30 minutes aboard a De Havilland Twin Otter freight plane. Tuk Tuk disappeared beneath us and the MacKenzie River Delta opened up—a vast plain pockmarked by stagnant ponds trapped above the permafrost. The place was flat except for mountainous pingos heaved up by frost. Tuk Tuk and Inuvik were just tiny specks in an immense wilderness of sky and land.

We retraced our route from Inuvik down the Dempster Highway. Near Milepost 450, three figures dotted the landscape: a Loucheux Indian caribou hunter, his grandson, and a dog carrying one of their packs.

We learned from the old man that he had been hunting the area all his life, waiting for the annual migration of the Porcupine River caribou herd. He said the deer could sense humanity and were afraid of the highway. It separated them from their calving grounds across the road.

When a truck came to pick them up three days later, the old man feared he would have to buy his meat this year from a grocery in Arctic Red River. He was very sad.

The Dempster Highway has become a symbol of progress. It is a bridge between the frontier and civilization. It represents the subjugation of the last great wilderness on the Northern continent. The land it cuts across is fragile. A bulldozer driver once carved his initials into the tundra while working on the road. The initials eroded and today are small ponds. Civilization tends to spread in much the same, thoughtless way.

We continued down the Dempster with a tape recorder and camera in search of people who live in the Yukon and Alaska. Some are natives. Others quit the South 48 in search of more independent lifestyles. All are what Jack Boone in this book calls the "real endangered species," unified in their isolation from the rest of the world.

—WLP

Down North

Bill Kowalchuk

MONEY CREEK, YUKON

BILL KOWALCHUK IS A SOURDOUGH. HE WAS BORN IN
1905 *and has watched the ice in the Canadian rivers break up
more than 60 times. He is known by the locations he prospected:
"Labrador Bill," "Hudson's Bay Bill," "Yellowknife Bill,"
and "Yukon Bill." An unfriendly encounter with a brown bear
left the old man with his present name, "One-Eyed Bill."*

*Kowalchuk has a claw scar on his left arm. The bones
are mended together around a surgical pin in his elbow. For pro-
tection, he keeps close by him a three-legged dog. He accidently
shot a leg off the dog while aiming, cock-eyed, at another bear.
Evenstill, the dog's bark insures that the sourdough will never
again be surprised in the woods by his cabin near Francis Lake.
The old man keeps a .45 magnum revolver on the table. He
refers fondly to it as his ".45 resolver." By the door is a loaded
.22 rifle.*

Kowalchuk pans alone for gold on Money Creek. The minerals he finds in the stream and in a claim staked out on his property are kept in buckets. He is a pan, pick, and shovel man living in an electronic age, a man who still works gravel through sluice boxes. He isolates ore with potatoes. Every few months he has the minerals trucked to a bank in Watson Lake which allows him a percentage of any profits.

Kowalchuk grouses at the world from under a worn Moose River hat, its brim well-fingered. It clashes with red longjohns and muddy boots. He dresses a little more formally when he ventures into Ben and Wilma's roadhouse to collect mail, dime novels, tobacco, rolling paper, and food.

Kowalchuk delights in unfragrant language. He acts tough, but beneath a gruff exterior he has a heart of gold.

"I wanted the gold and I got it—
   Came out with a fortune last fall,
Yet somehow life's not what I thought it,
   And somehow the gold isn't all."

—ROBERT SERVICE, *"The Spell of the Yukon"*

"Gold is heavy but it rises to the top."

OLD RUSSIAN PROVERB

2 0

"I'M A SOURDOUGH.

"A prospector is an educated S.O.B. who works on the theories given to him in school. They come into the country and starve 'cause they don't know what to look for.

"A sourdough is a guy who has stuck it out for a season and has seen the ice go out of the rivers. They're hardy like sourdough bread. They keep for a long time. They come out of the country with the yallar stuff in their hands. That's a sourdough.

"I came into the country and taught myself to do everything. Built the cabin we're sitting in and invented gumbo to fill chinks in between the logs. Gumbo sticks to the sides of my cabin like wet shit sticks to dry pants.

"I built my own sluice boxes, my own generators, and the bridge that spans the creek. Even invented my own mineral theory on how to locate gold and learned to use potatoes to isolate it. I am one of the Seven Wonders of the World. They call me a legend. I think I'm more of an experience.

"To find gold I study geographically the lay of the land. Now, there's such a thing as *ingenious* rock. The earth is one big boulder of ingenious rock. The surface of it is badly mauled from volcanoes and glaciers, like my body with its bear scratches and gun shot wounds. In the bowels of this earth is gold, just as there is a heart in my body, geographically speakin'.

"Now, I know that water washed in the early stages of

life eons ago. With it came gold. Gold follows the water. Yukon gold here on Money Creek might have washed in from the Himalayas or the Amazon, from Alexandria or Arabia. Water never sits still because the earth rotates. The same bucket of water that leaves Baffin Island turns up later in the Bering Straits. With it comes the gold.

"I know from 60 years of prospectin' where gold from the bowels of the earth is. I also know how trees grow. Certain symptoms and mucous serps force their way up through roots, ferment like whiskey, and send syrups into the sprouts, buds, leaves, and needles of trees. Then they congeal and die.

"Same with minerals like gold. All the different minerals fermented early on. They mixed like the ingredients of a cake. Flour, butter, sugar, milk. They oozed their way to the earth's surface and congealed in layers. Gold, platinum, silver, zinc. That may be too *deep* for you. But I'm telling ya. As a botanist.

"I chose to work Money Creek here. Gold washes in from the Liard and Yukon rivers before it drains off into the Arctic Sea. I've taken 12 steps following that gold from Labrador to Old Crow. I've just kept moving, following the rivers, hooked by the idea that life is always greener over the next bend. What I didn't realize until recently was that there's a car coming over the next bend. When you meet, there'll be a crash.

"You see, gold has always fascinated men. It goes back to ancient Persia, to the Romans and Chinese. Three wise men rode on camels laden with rubies, diamonds, and gold. Right? GOLD. It hooks ya.

"Looking for gold is a gamble. Look at it this way. You've got a dollar in your pocket. You're walking down the street, and you hear the call of a barker giving ya two-to-one odds if you can guess which hand a coin's under.

"You guess, 'That hand.' The barker tells you you're right. You was watchin' and won an extra dollar. You didn't think that the guy was a con man fishin' for ya. And you didn't know that he was hiding other coins between his fingers.

"You get hooked in your confidence and bet both dollars next time. You may win again before he gets you. Then you lose and lose big. That's the twelfth step. It's the damn world today. Your greed takes over and you try the card game once more. Same with gold fever.

"I don't search far anymore. I've stopped here at Money Creek. I'm content to make enough to buy my own whiskey, have a squaw every now and then, and read my novels. I scrawl poetry on the walls when I get bored. I eat well. I have my dog, my health, and 210 pounds of mineral worth $8,000-a-ton stacked up in the shed. I'm my own damn boss out here.

"I've seen all kinds of things that go on in the world. You guys on the hardtops and pavement with your bright lights and bars, police, and schoolin' can't see what *I* see. Greed. Jealousy. Wheelin' and dealing. You're blinded by the lights, Mr. Man. I'm not."

Merl Martin

WATSON LAKE, YUKON

MERL MARTIN HAS ONE OF THE YUKON'S GREAT BEARDS. *He has fractured his wrist, broken his back, lost a few teeth, and claims he can still feel the tip of a finger amputated after a bout with frostbite. What remains intact is his mind—and a vast reserve of memorized Robert Service poetry.*

The poetry could have been written about Martin. Born in 1917, he left Alberta with his father to homestead in the Yukon. They trapped, hunted, fished, and prospected, finding just enough of everything to subsist and large doses of freedom.

Martin never struck it rich and today squats on Crown Land in a trailer outside Watson Lake. His common-law wife is Lucy Ellen, a Tlingit woman who shoots game with a .22 rifle to supplement their diet of canned food.

A natural raconteur, the prospector shares some of his adventures between recitations of Service poetry, bannock bread, and coffee.

26

"I WAS BORN IN 1917 AND CAME INTO THE BUSH WITH MY Dad at the age of 12. We built a cabin on Grist Lake and lived on caribou meat, moose, bannock, flour, and tea. We brought in six horses, but in six cold weeks they got bogged down in terrible weather. By the end of our first winter we had to shoot the whole works.

"The next time we went in we took dogs. They had a quarter timber wolf in 'em mixed with Saint Bernard and Newfoundland. One dog weighed 152 pounds. His legs were bigger than my arms. With him and three others we could haul up to 800 pounds of gear when we went cutting wood, trapping, or trading at the Hudson's Bay post.

"We taught ourselves to trap. I got my first silver fox as a kid in 1929. They were quite rare. He was frozen, and I was trying to thaw him out. I warmed him up a little too fast, and a small singe mark appeared. I tried to work it out with my fingers, but the old fur buyer at the trading post put it across his arm and held it to the light. He'd been in the business for a while I guess.

"I would have gotten $500 for that silver fox pelt. Because of that singe mark, the price was knocked down to $300. I say knocked down, but that was still a lot of money back in the Depression. I heard of one Aleut who trapped four silver fox puppies alive back then. He was offered $20,000 by the Hudson's Bay Company to breed them. They come out all silver for three generations.

"When I was growing up I used to strike off along a

12-day trapline by the Buffalo River for 60 miles. I built five cabins along that line and could cover from 10 to 40 miles a day with dogs. For food I shot my own game. I sometimes went off for five months without seeing a soul. Talked to myself and to the dogs a lot. Sometimes came back barking like a dog myself. It sounds funny when you start talking with people again.

"Anyway, I was once scared by wolves. I was 12, and my Dad and I was out hunting moose. He went off calling one just as it was getting dark and told me to build a fire. So I'm alone cutting kindling when this damn great big white timber wolf comes out of the bush.

"I climbed a tree but was so scared that I fell out. Then I grabbed a stick and started to cry. In the meantime, this wolf sits down nearby, cocks his head and looks at me. I could hear others howling to the north as I ran away. We could hear them around us all that night baying."

"The toughest animal I ever came across was the wolverine. I once caught one in my traps in Madison Creek and shot it three times with a .30/06. Once through the shoulder, once through the hip, and in the front legs, breaking them. And *still* he growled at me, jumping around with his hind feet. Finally I shot him through the neck. He was growling when I fetched him on the ice. I had to beat him over the head to finish him off. They're tough.

"I knew of a priest at Ross River who once found a wolverine in his trap-line cache. He was stupid enough to go in there and close the door behind him. Luckily he killed the animal with one blow of his axe.

"Moose aren't the best things to shoot for sport. They usually just stand there and look at you. Still, I once had to shoot one. I was prospecting up in the Yukon north of Ross River around 1973. I had almost run out of food and was waiting for a plane to take me and the paydirt out when I spotted a great big bull moose in rut with three cows. I teased him, calling across the lake. He'd come out to shore and grunt at me. I did this a few times.

"The plane didn't come in that day due to snow so the next day, I returned to the same spot with my dogs and set up a campfire. I don't know what made me look back just as I got the fire started, but there was this bull moose standing there looking at me. He got up on his hind feet. Then he come for me. Must have wanted to run me out of the country for teasing him.

"I reached over and grabbed one of my bigger dogs by the collar, but he kept coming, bellowin'. I let go of the dog and fired with a .30/06 from where I stood.

"When it was over I looked at that big bugger. He weighed about 1,600 pounds. His tongue stickin' out was the length of my arm.

"Well, I put up some water for tea and just as it come to a boil, I hear an airplane landing. That pilot was shocked when he saw that moose layin' there. We skinned it out, took him back with us, and that was that."

"Bears are remarkable. They can run about 40 miles per hour and come at you fast for such a big creature. You try to shoot them in the chest to bring them down. Neck shots are okay too but only if they're straight on. There's a nerve center there that knocks the feet from under 'em. It's weird. When you skin them out, they look almost humanoid with huge biceps, triceps, and skeletal features like some ape man.

"The way you tell the difference between black bears and brown grizzlies is that the black bears will climb a tree after you, and the grizzlies will knock the tree down. On the whole the black bears are less dangerous.

"Still, I recall hearing about an Indian boy who was killed by a black bear recently. He came across one with his father, eating on a moose. The boy decided to go after this bear and left the moose with his Dad. It got to be sundown, and the old man heard a bear roarin' his head off in the nearby spruce. From the sound of things he knew that his boy had had it.

"In the morning a search party traced the boy's trail, following the bear tracks along a deer path. They saw that as the boy came out under a spruce stand, the bear ambushed him and grabbed him in the back of the neck. He never even got a chance to fire his gun.

"I heard of a guy killing a bear with a hunting knife once, but he lost his arm in the deal. He was stalked and caught so he held out his arm for the bear to chew on while he cut into the bear's stomach with his free hand. Once a bear loses its guts, it gives up the fight. The man's arm was chewed up enough that it had to be amputated. Same sort of thing happened recently to a woman geologist in the bush. She lost both arms and both legs. She managed to call for help on a walkie talkie, and a helicopter picked her up."

Ralph Troberg

DAWSON CITY, YUKON

AT THE TURN OF THE CENTURY, CRIES OF "GOLD!"
*echoed from Dawson City to Nome. Thousands of Stampeders
rushed into the hills from the South 48 to stake their claims. Gold
fever was running high—many died while in their delirium.*

*Alaska and the Yukon have been stories of boom and bust,
with gold prices riding a rollercoaster. As recently as 1980,
values soared to more than $500 an ounce. Old dredge sites and
tailing piles were reworked by modern mineral corporations.*

*The heyday of Dawson City, however, remains fixed in
the public imagination around the Gay '90s, in creeks named
Bonanza, Eldorado, and Eureka. Less successful legacies also dot
the map: Too Little Gold Creek, Deadman's Gulch, Jackass
Canyon, Last Chance, and No Grub.*

*Today, Dawson's gold isn't found in creeks but in credit
cards—Visa, MasterCard, and Diners Club. Tourists are*

bussed in to gawk at rusting dredges, rotting steamboats, and professional dance girls who—for the price of a ticket—perform the cancan in aseptic surroundings.

Ralph Troberg remembers the place differently. His father came across the Chilkoot Pass with the early stampeders. The family was raised in a more exciting Dawson.

Troberg, who was born in 1905, talks about the Gold Rush and the disillusionment of working much of his life on dredges in Hunker, Eldorado, and Bonanza creeks. He sits rocking on a porch at the Dawson Pioneer Home for retired people. The tourist buses go by in a cloud of dust, too busy to stop for the real thing.

"There's a race of men that don't fit in,
A race that can't stay still;
So they break the hearts of kith and kin,
And roam the world at will."

—ROBERT SERVICE, *"The Men That Don't Fit In"*

"My father came from Finland to New York on a windjammer haulin' lumber in 1893. He jumped ship and come to Seattle by train. There he met the woman who was to become my mother. He didn't marry her until 1900 when he had made enough money prospecting in Dawson to come back outside and claim her.

"In 1894 my old man was in Alaska tunneling under the sea for quartz off Douglas Island. Word spread of Klondike gold. In 1897 he set off for the Chilkoot Pass and Dawson to strike it rich.

"My father didn't have $500 or 1,000 pounds of grub with him. He was caught by the Canadian police who used to weigh in men before letting them cross the Chilkoot Pass. The police also confiscated all revolvers. Only rifles were allowed. Handguns were kept in a local jail and returned when the stampeders left. This kept the murder rate down.

"To make enough money to buy food my father and a partner named Christenson went into business. They hauled supplies through the Chilkoot for greenhorn doctors and lawyers. They packed 70-pound sacks across the Pass four times a day for 49 cents a pound. Dad was just 19 when a whole bunch of these greenhorns died in a Chilkoot avalanche. You can still see their unnamed wooden grave markers in Dyea, marked 'died, April 3, 1898.' Soon after that Dad had enough food and money to press on.

"From Dawson City, Dad went up to Indian River, 30 miles north of town. Didn't find nothing there so he re-

turned to the mouth of Hunker Creek to pan with Harry Jones, an Australian. He worked for 20 years on the dredges after that, up and down the creek beds.

"In the meantime my Old Man married. He never made any real money. Just enough to keep looking for more gold. You get hooked.

"When I grew up, I worked on the dredges like my Old Man for 45 cents an hour on Bonanza and El Dorado creeks. These dredges scraped up bedrock with a huge shovel. The stuff was dumped into buckets on a pulley. The buckets went onto a hopper. From there, the gold was sorted in huge sluices on either side of the dredge. Like my father, I managed to go broke four times mining on my own. Each time I returned to work on these dredges.

"When times were good, I managed to take out about $5,000 in gold a year. That was on Bonanza Creek in the 1920s. Gold was going for $15.70 an ounce when I started. It reached as high as $35 an ounce when I quit in 1935. I thought I had the world by the tail. Now I look at its price, and it's over $300 an ounce.

"In 1938 I returned to Bonanza with a partner and a 400-horsepower pump. We left a tailing pile almost a mile long. Beat working in the mining camps 12 hours a day for $5.40. Today the same sort of work brings in $14 an hour, but I'm too old and wise to get back into it.

"I never expected to hit it rich you know. It was just the love of finding gold in your pan. When you turned off your pump and saw gold lying in the sluice box ripples, that was a mighty good feeling.

"You know, gold is funny. It grips you even though half of the Johnny-come-lately's never made a cent. A lot of fellas were drifters, following the stampedes down the rivers.

They lived in tents and built cabins on rafts with cookstoves. Some came from the Juneau and Vancouver rushes to lose out in Dawson in '98. After Bonanza 20,000 sourdoughs left for the beaches of Nome. The Yukon River current was below the surface; so these rafters would attach barrels of rocks to the gunwales. They'd heave the barrels overboard, and the current would carry them downstream all the way to Saint Michaels. Those that slept missed the whistles of the steamboats. Sometimes they got hit in the night and were never heard from again. After Nome in 1905, the Fairbanks Stampede hit. These same gold-struck drifters took off again. Yup. Because of gold, people was always going like hell and gettin' no place.

"I remember growing up in Dawson at the turn of the century. It was a pretty big place. Maybe 35,000 people. Before the Rush there couldn't have been more than 400 people living in tents and log cabins. Now the town's gone back down to about 1,000 year 'rounders. Like most towns in Alaska and the Yukon, Dawson boomed and busted.

"Gold made Dawson. I remember as a boy in the Rush days how men used to pay for supplies and grub with gold. They would carry it around with them and have it weighed out at the Bank of Commerce where Robert Service used to work.

"I knew some fellows who got the job of raising the floor of the old Bank of Commerce for some renovation work. They found all kinds of gold that had slipped down through the floorboards as clerks were weighing it. Those workers got more from this gold than from their renovation work.

"The Dawson saloons were quite something during the gold rush. I remember being a paper boy in 1910. I wasn't

supposed to go into these saloons, but I did. The places were full of drunks and prospectors, fighting over things they forgot about by the end of the evening. The jails were also full. Back then the policemen had calluses on their feet. Now they have calluses on their asses.

"I remember when they voted the booze out of saloons in 1921. That didn't work a damn. All people had to do was to cough coming up the stairs to see the doctor. He'd write out a medicinal prescription for a bottle of booze for you to hand to the government liquor vendor.

"Dawson was a hard place for women to live in back then. There were no flush toilets. The streets weren't paved. There were no telephones. If there was a meeting at one of the hotels, they raised a flag. For insulation in winter saloons had horseshit around the pipes. It was tough for the women.

"I remember taking the steamer *Dawson* to Whitehorse in 1925. She was the last boat of the season. Hit a rock while loaded with 250 of us onboard. Her boiler stuck in the sand, and the back end of the vessel sunk underwater. That's how she stayed.

"Well, the mate cried out, 'Women and children off first.' I remember that before the women and children they unloaded the barge in tow laden with unrefined ore and gold.

"Once everyone was unloaded safely we got a hold of a Model-T Ford truck. It was up to us men to ride to Whitehorse for help. Unfortunately we had the 'Spot Cash Kid' with us. He was loaded with white wine. He used to run the taxi in Dawson, and you had to pay cash when he landed you. Even if your girlfriend was along, if you didn't have cash *on the spot,* he'd beat the shit out of you. That's how he got his name.

"Anyway, we managed to get 10 miles with the Kid driving and drinking when he swerved off a sharp curve and into the woods. It was hours before a blacksmith could come in from Carmacks and bend back the radius rod and wheels.

"The Kid got us another 10 miles down the road before turning the truck over into the side of a hill. One fella got hurt. His glasses cut into his cheek.

"From there we walked the final 10 miles into Carmacks. In town there was a free meal waiting for us at the roadhouse. One old-timer from Sixty-Mile removed a chair from the table. He said, 'It was the thirteenth when the *Dawson* foundered. There was 13 of us on that truck. And I'll be damned if I'll sit down to this table with 13 chairs.'

"From Carmacks, we got to Whitehorse by mailtruck. No one would let Spot Cash drive. We made it with hard-boiled eggs, sandwiches, and a bottle of rum owned by the

Commissioner that he salvaged from the boat. They sent down 11 cars to fetch the women and children. No one got a cent of compensation from the steamship company that owned the *Dawson*."

"I used to have a 'bear dog' when I was driving Cats while constructing the Dempster Highway. Whenever that dog saw a bear, he would run over to bite it in the ass.

"One day a damned bear came along while I was working in a ditch, and this dog gets it. Well, that was fine. But the next thing the dog did invariably was to run back to me with its tail between its legs and the bear close behind. I had to stand there with a shovel ready to wang the bear if he got near. Fortunately the bear ran off the ditch bank before he got to me.

"Sometimes I would crawl on my hands and knees like a bear. That dog would come to bite *me* in the ass. That was quite a dog. Braver than hell."

41

G. I. Cameron

WHITEHORSE, YUKON

G. I. CAMERON JOINED THE ROYAL CANADIAN MOUNTED *Police in the days when they patrolled the Yukon on horseback and with dog sled teams. Today the RCMP is more likely to use aircraft or patrol cars.*

Cameron was born in Quebec in 1900. After serving in the army, he became a narcotics officer with the Vancover, B.C. police. He welcomed the opportunity to patrol the remote territory around Selkirk, Yukon and lived in a wilderness cabin with his wife and with a daughter who would grow up to become Yukon's first woman commissioner.

Today Cameron lives comfortably in a house in Whitehorse, a city by Yukon's standards. He tells about his days of derring-do with refined understatement, a telltale eyebrow arching over frosty hazel eyes when he wishes to underscore a particularly lurid detail.

"I used to cover the patrols on my own. In summer the steamboats were the best way to travel from Whitehorse to Selkirk. I used to put my small boat right on the steamers, and from there, patrol up all the side streams. It was a grand way to see the Yukon and its scenery.

"I remember the *Klondike II* before she became a floating museum in Whitehorse. She had the very best of everything from service to food. As a policeman, I got to know all the crew, captains, and pilots. They knew their rivers pretty well, but once in a while, they'd find themselves run aground on a bar.

"To get off a sandbar the steamships used 'deadmen.' A deadman was a huge log which would be buried four feet down in a trench. Cables were run from the log to the steamer. They'd winch the boats off.

"Steamships also used to have big grasshopper-like legs attached to their gunwales. They could use these legs to pole-vault over bars, walking on logs sunk into the sand below.

"When the nights got cold in fall, steamboat paddle wheels had to be thawed out with steam in the mornings to get the vessels off the bars. Some boats were caught in the ice and had to be abandoned through the winter.

"I was once on board a steamer when it ran aground. We were about 90 yards from the Selkirk landing when one of the huge pistons slipped. The whole piston head blew out through the deck. It missed a friend of mine by inches, saving him the displeasure of being cut in half. The boat came to a dead stop.

"I was up in the wheelhouse with the captain at the time. He swung her into the current, and we drifted downstream with a full load of ore. The crew tried to stop us by

throwing a cable around the trees on shore, but the weight of the vessel tore the trees out. Finally, we hit a bar and ran aground in a slough. As the local policeman, I got in a canoe and paddled back to Selkirk to report the incident.

"On another trip to Selkirk I was startled in the middle of the night by the steamer's whistle. Everyone crowded on deck to witness one of the great caribou herds crossing the river by the thousands. We just cut engines and drifted through them all night.

"The steamships used to carry ore down the Yukon River. Miners' pay dirt was piled on the banks for a quarter of a mile—nothing but 125-pound bags of ore stacked up. It was loaded on barges by husky college boys. These loaders made $35 a month and got to see the Yukon to boot. Then it was all floated down the Stewart River to Mayo and loaded on the steamships. From there, it went to the smugglers on

leaving, I heard an awful commotion coming from that barn. The dogs in the corner had just enough lead in their lines to get to the dog in the middle. Because they were jealous of the lead dog, and because he was no match for four of them, they tore him apart. He was disemboweled by the time I got back. I had to shoot him to put him out of his misery.

"These were big huskies. Each weighed from 90 to 100 pounds. They had all kinds of things mixed in including wolf. They were probably as strong as Buck that Jack London wrote about in *The Call of the Wild*. These weren't your tame dogs, although I always treated them well. They were half wild.

"When I was out on the trail, I always stayed with the trappers. You were always welcome. You would come in after a day of mushing, all tired, and they would help you put away your dogs. Then they'd give you a few shots of rum. All you'd want to do by then was go to sleep. All they'd want to do was talk. Catch up on gossip in town, you know.

"Sometimes, I'd come upon a trapper's cabin, and the man would be dead by the stream. Frozen. If they died of natural causes, I had to bury them. If there was any question of foul play, I had to take 'em in to the coroner for an autopsy.

"Burying dead men wasn't the worst thing I had to do on my patrols. It was handling drunken women. That was the worst. Sometimes had to roll the larger ones onto the sled and take them into town to sober up. Boy, some of them women got to be big!

"One funny experience I had was when I was on inspection detail in the 1930s at the Yukon River. I was stationed at the docks to inspect the boats coming in for stolen ore. It was Prohibition in the States, and this one boatload of Americans saw me. In an instant, they unloaded all of their hootch and moonshine over the side. When I told them what I was looking for, and that there was no Prohibition in Canada, they were a sorry-looking crew!

"Dog sledding and horse-drawn buggies went out of fashion when the airplanes entered the scene. I used to fly around with all of Canada's best and not-so-best bush pilots. We flew mostly in Fairchilds—the workhorse of the North. They took mail and police on the rounds to Dawson and Fort McPherson. We also carried freight and supplies into the Territory.

"I remember it was Christmas Eve, and I had to get from Whitehorse to Carmacks. No planes were flying, and it was minus 70 degrees.

"My pilot says, 'Do you want to go?'

"I says 'It's up to you.'

"He decided to go, and told me to get into the plane, a Beechcraft. This was in the late 1930s. I lay down on some mail sacks, and we took off into a sky filled with the northern lights. The whole place was just sparkling.

"Well, things went okay until we reached just over Carmacks. The engine started to splutter and cough. Then it quit altogether.

"The pilot says, 'Don't look so white, Cameron. If we hit the ground, I'll be the first to die.' This was little consolation to me. Just as we were starting to lose altitude, the engine caught on again. That was okay, but the throttle had frozen wide open. We hit some stumps at the end of the runway. They clipped the wings off, but we weren't hurt.

"We had Christmas dinner at the Carmacks telegraph office that night with the line man. It was an expensive operation for the owner of that plane."

Ida May Mack Goulter

CARMACKS, YUKON

IDA MAY MACK IS A YUKON PIONEER. SHE WAS BORN IN
*1893 and grew up in Dawson City during the Klondike Stam-
pede. She claims to have danced with Robert Service, the poet,
when he was living in Dawson. She has never ventured further
than Carmacks, known then as Tantalus.*

*Mack married Frank Goulter, Sr., who died in 1981 at
the age of 104. She points to a plaque on the wall signed by
Queen Victoria to her husband "For Service in the Boer Wars."
He was a member of the Royal Artillery.*

*Goulter, as Mack calls her husband, joined the Northwest
Mounted Police in 1903 and helped recapture Earnest Cashiel, a
notorious murderer who was later convicted and hanged. He came
to patrol Yukon Crossing and Tantalus for a dollar a day and
met his future wife. They supplemented his income raising mink
and foxes, trapping, and fishing.*

Mack still lives in a log cabin she helped build in 1910 with her husband and her son, Frank Goulter, Jr., who retired from a career of cutting wood for the old steamboats that plied the Yukon River.

Inside the cabin are collections of stuffed wolverines, birds, and mink—the efforts of Goulter, Sr., who took up taxidermy in his later years. Orchids and butterflies are preserved in glass cases.

For more than 25 years, Mack kept a journal of her life which she titled "Jawboning." She keeps the handwritten, yellowed pages stored in a musty trunk in one of the back rooms of the house. Excerpts from her journal follow.

"This is the law of the Yukon,
that only the strongest shall thrive;
That surely the Weak shall perish,
and only the Fit survive.
Dissolute, damned and despairful,
crippled and palsied and slain,
This is the Will of the Yukon,
Lo, how she makes it plain!"

—ROBERT SERVICE, *"The Law of the Yukon"*

"I HAVE LIVED FOR NEARLY A CENTURY IN THE YUKON and have watched an entire generation of gold stampeders disappear. I am the last of the Mack family alive. I was born in Minneapolis, Minnesota, in 1893.

"The legacy of Yukon's pioneers will live on in the creeks, rivers, and towns. Names such as Dawson, McQuesten, Harper, Mayo, Ladue, Laberge, Hunker, Henderson, and Carmacks will never die. So too will the perilous history reflected in creek names such as Little Gold, No Gold, Too Much Gold, All Gold, Eureka, Bonanza, Opher, Sulphur, and Eldorado, which, in Mexican, means 'the gold is here.'

"My own people, the Macks, have history that lives on in creek names. My people worked a tributary that came to be known as Mack Fork. Today, that is the name that appears on mining maps of the area around where we live in Carmacks. The highest mountain in the Carmacks area has been named Goulter Mountain, after my husband, the late Frank Goulter, Sr.

"Other places have been named for my family. Dolly Creek was named for me. For my sister, Victoria, is Victoria Creek and Mountain. For my father, Cortlandt, is Cortlandt Creek and for my brother is Kirkland Creek. Gold claims are named for my sister and daughter—Hazel and Anne. My mother, May, and my sister, Hazel, had lakes and a valley named for them around 1903.

"To prevent the names of my family from disappearing, I now mention the four Mack brothers: Cortlandt (Cort)

Ida May Mack Goulter (second from right), 1946.
Private photo.

days. On the whole, many women withstood the isolation better than the men.

"There were gold-seekers other than prospectors in Dawson who preferred to sit back and let gold come to them. In addition to the saloon-keepers and traders there were the dance hall girls.

"Though in no way pioneers in the sense that respectable married women were, the dance hall girls of Dawson do have a right to be numbered among the old-timers.

"The red-light district of Dawson was around Second Avenue. A rougher quarter was in Klondike City across the Yukon River, known as 'Louse Town.' This was an area occupied by the coarser women as opposed to the dance hall girls.

"The dance hall girls were no more straight-laced than their fellow sisters-of-joy, but they were generally young, pretty, and had ladylike manners. They were primarily engaged as entertainers who could sing and render sad ballads. These touched the sad, homesick hearts of miners who would weep, cheer, and throw nuggets at the girls' feet. On stage, the girls wore black, Parisian outfits, tight-fitting above the waist with a short, flared skirt showing frothy underwear and long, black stockings. I remember how their garters often flashed real diamond buckles, not rhinestones. Often their jewelry was pure gold.

"The dance halls and saloons were magnets to attract men who had spent months and even years in solitude. Miners were often prepared to pay lavishly for a smile and an hour of female companionship.

"Many of the girls cashed in on the Yukon Stampede and became extremely wealthy. The charge for a waltz partner was one dollar paid to the house in advance at the bar.

The dance would be just long enough to circle the floor once when it came time for the miner to buy the girl a drink. The girl got a cut on each drink that she persuaded a man to buy.

"On average, it took $100 to entertain a girl for an hour. She would order a bottle and, depending upon the size of a man's poke, she'd see that none was left. If her partner was too sober, she'd weep a little and spin a hard luck yarn as to how she needed money for this or that.

"As the night went by, the girls would retire to their rooms and put on kimonos. Charges were based on the time a man spent upstairs with a girl. The girls were free from disease, being inspected regularly by doctors except in 'Louse Town' down the street. There were few complaints and business was conducted with no undue noise. Most of the girls' fees went to the house.

"The best of the dance halls was the Flora Dora, owned by Murray Eades. The girls received up to $200 a month for room and board. The lobby sported real leather chairs and couches. The walls were decorated with life-size paintings of nude women. Above was a balcony used by the girls to inspect prospects and invite them up.

"Some of the 'lady prostitutes' were real gold diggers. They enjoyed a clientele of men with bulging gold pokes and an ability to write gift cheques to the value of not less than $1,000. Many miners were broken in health and bankroll by girls who demanded expensive Christmas presents.

"Many girls didn't make fortunes. They were paid wages of $100 a week plus room and board in some of the halls. They were allowed to keep all presents of gold and jewels. They looked forward to the day when they could make enough money to leave or to marry into respectable, anonymous lives outside.

headway against the Yukon current. Sometimes, to prevent her from going backwards, the crew had to feed better-quality wood to the burners to get an extra burst of speed around a point.

"One fall the *Flying* ran aground on a bar in the Pelly River. She never moved again. Her cargo had to be unloaded and packed out 70 miles on the backs of men and dogs.

"The steamboat trade was not without its tragedies. I recall the calm, sunny afternoon of September 26, 1906. I heard a heavy explosion up-river and saw a cloud of white smoke rising over the trees. Cort also heard the explosion and felt his cabin shake.

"My father and I saw the steamer *Columbian* turn into a flaming wreck. Some black powder kegs on the vessel had ignited, creating an explosion of such force that much of her cargo was blown clear across the river. This included thousands of apples, slabs of bacon and salt pork, hams, and cheeses. My father gathered some lovely looking apples. Cutting them open, their insides were filled with black powder. Nothing left was fit for human consumption.

"Six men lost their lives in the explosion. Walsh, the mate, was drowned. His body was found near Rink Rapids by the trappers Prisick, Olds, and Cottle. They shot a lynx feeding on the corpse and sent the hide to the dead mate's mother. She returned the hide saying that she needed no such souvenir by which to remember her son.

"Others like Cowper, the purser, were badly burned. He died later in Whitehorse after losing his mind from the mental and physical agony he suffered.

"The *Klondyke* struck a wall near Jack Knife Bend and became a total loss. Her cargo proved happy hunting grounds for the river folk. For 200 miles along the Yukon, women who could talk from personal experience about events which placed them close to 100 years of age. Yet these old folks were swept away when the whites came in, bringing with them influenza which hit the Yukon in epidemic proportions in 1916.

"The lot of Indian women was hard. Their hands were never idle as they squatted on crossed legs, sewing and dressing furs.

"I recall one Indian squaw near her time to have a baby reaching my father's camp. She and her husband were trappers headed for the trading post at Little Salmon. The squaw had an enormous pack on her back in addition to a baby strapped to a shoe in front. The man carried only a small bag containing cartridges and his rifle.

"When the woman reached my father, she groaned. My father asked, 'Squaw have baby soon?' Her husband nodded for her. They started to head off again when my father stopped them, threatening to call the police if they moved on.

"The Indian husband consented to camp a short distance from the cabin. The squaw immediately put the year-old baby on the ground and started to cut small spruce trees for their camp. That evening she gave birth to a baby boy. The next morning they would have gone on immediately to Little Salmon had my father not insisted that they remain another two days in camp.

"When an Indian woman was having a baby all the family watched the delivery. The only obstetric aid was a short stick driven into the ground for the woman to pull on. Many squaws died in childbirth as well as their infants. The Indians did not bury stillborn babies. On many occasions I have noticed a small bundle tied to a tall

pole high up in a spruce tree. Once I asked an Indian woman what it contained. She said she did not know. When I made it clear that I would find out for myself she hurriedly begged me not to touch the bundle. It contained a dead baby. Only since the coming of whites did this practice discontinue.

"In winter, because of the permafrost, it was Indian practice to wrap their adult dead in hides, placed on racks above ground. It was only a matter of time before squirrels tore the hides to pieces. In summer shallow graves were dug into the east sides of hills. Small houses were constructed over the bodies. Into these houses were placed cooking utensils and artifacts for the convenience of the dead person's final journey to the Great Spirit.

"Nothing that had belonged to a dead person was ever used again. Even a cabin where the death occurred would be abandoned. I once told an Indian that I would like to have a pair of snowshoes that I had seen hanging in a tree over two summers. The next time I passed that way they had been removed. I later learned that they had belonged to a dead man.

"When an Indian killed a moose or caribou the whole band would travel to the kill and eat until they could eat no more. What was left of the carcass was packed out by the dogs.

"The dogs were grossly overloaded and abused with sticks. Many collapsed and died with their packs on. When this occurred the back pack was never touched again by the Indians. A small shallow grave would be scraped out next to the dead animal and both the pack and dog would be shoved in. No Indian would venture near that spot again, even after the carcass was consumed by other animals. I have seen frying pans, cups, and plates lying abandoned by these burial places.

"Years ago Indians would not kill a bear. Many believed that they had been reincarnated from bears.

"I remember the story of two Little Salmon Indians determined to hunt out a bear. Good John was an old man, nearly 90, and Crazy Frank was in his 20s. They spotted steam issuing from a shallow den on a hillside and were convinced there was a brown bear in it (grizzly).

"Good John took a long pole and jabbed it inside the den. A large brown bear rushed out through the leaves and grass it had stored for warmth. Dazzled by the daylight it missed Good John and charged Crazy Frank who had a .45/90 rifle.

"Crazy Frank dropped the gun and sprinted to the nearest tree leaving Good John to defend himself with the pole. As the bear started to climb the tree after Crazy Frank, John reached for the gun. The bear changed its mind and charged. Good John fired into the bear's open mouth and the bear dropped. The men ran away.

"When the Indians returned the next day, they dug out the bear's eyes, 'So the bear could not see who killed him.' Good John was quite sincere in the belief that the bear might be the spirit of an old enemy killed in a tribal feud. Only after the eyes were out did the old man skin out that bear and bring the meat and hide home.

"Many of the Indians that I knew were trappers. They would go to the Little Salmon trading post to sell their furs. Some of the traders made fortunes by swindling Indians.

"Very little actual cash changed hands. Traders bartered tokens and trade money. When the Big Lake Indians came in on the spring trek with furs, the factor of the Little

Salmon trading post would have each man lay out his catch along the counter, one fur at a time. A price would be offered which the Indian had to accept. There was no place else to trade.

"The Indians would buy blankets, clothing, calico, guns and cartridges, tea, and sugar. They would be lucky to get as much as ten silver dollars in cash to balance furs worth many hundreds of dollars. This, plus a drink of strong brewed tea, was the Indian's reward for a winter of hard work.

"There was a strong code of honesty among the Indians in the old days. If an Indian didn't have money to pay for certain goods at the trading post, he would 'jawbone' or 'pay on tick.' This meant that he would be given credit until he could pay at another time. The old Indians always paid what they owed.

"Once Crazy Frank brought a fine fox pelt for my father. Cort complimented him and offered to pay, but the Indian said, 'No mine. Yours. Wolverine come by.' He had seen the wolverine and knew that if he didn't remove the dead fox it would be torn to pieces. He returned it to the owner of the trap.

"In the winter of 1904, Chief Joseph of the Tatchen Creek tribe was on his way to Little Salmon. He met Cort and family and showed them an empty tin of condensed milk, saying, 'No steal em. Just take Babee.' Cort smiled and said it was all right for the Chief to take milk for his baby. Several months later the Chief returned. He brought Cort a piece of caribou meat.

"The Indians never forgot a kindness, but now they have changed to white man's ways."

"Early settlers and prospectors named the creeks after

animals: *Marten, Fish, Bear, Wolverine, Porcupine, Ottertail, Wolf, King Salmon, Crow, Goose, Ptarmigan, Grouse, Caribou, Fox, Moose, Beaver, Whale, Seal, Owl,* and *Mosquito.* Most people living in the North have had some encounter or experience to share about their wild brethren.

"Caribou are harmless and gentle. The magnificent woodland caribou is a thing of beauty when standing as a sentinel. Many people have seen the regal, majestic Osborn caribou, mistaking it for the woodland breed. The barren-land caribou migrate in huge herds across the tundra. They do not crowd together like herds of buffalo, horses, or cattle. Although fast, they are fully aware of their surroundings. I have never heard of anyone getting trampled by caribou herds.

"My father told me how in the spring of 1930 he was on a patch of treeless hillside. He saw the whole other side of the valley in motion. He thought he must be suffering from dizziness or some optical illusion when he realized that the movement was a caribou herd coming right toward him.

"There was no shelter and no time to get out of the way so he just stood there waiting to be trampled. As the herd reached him they separated. Not one animal touched him nor did they bump into other animals.

"After awhile my father got tired and just sat down. It was five hours before the continuous stream of animals thinned sufficiently for him to make camp two miles away.

"No one at the camp believed my father when he related his experience, but a similar thing happened near Stewart. A father had gone out to tend a small garden by his cabin. His three-year-old son was with him and wandered off apiece. By the time the father heard the herd of caribou, they had reached the boy. All sight of him was blotted out.

"The man was so shaken from the supposed death of his son that he fainted. He came to as the last of the caribou were passing, looked up, and saw the little boy running toward him, untouched. He was crying 'bad doggies.'

"My son, Frank Jr., must be one of the few people who have ever experienced a ride on the back of a wild caribou. He was 15 and shot a male with big antlers. He left his gun on the snow and bent over to cut the beast's throat. (Caribou must be dressed within 15 minutes of death. The animals have a high temperature, and the meat and stomach contents sour rapidly.)

"Well, Frankie bestrode the fallen animal's neck, holding the knife with one hand and an antler with the other when the caribou came to. It sprang to its feet. In an instant my son found himself moving at top speed astride a terrified animal. He bounced off, tumbling and rolling. From then on he shot his game twice, 'To make certain it was dead.'

"The cream-colored grizzly (tundra bear) is extremely rare and very beautiful. I doubt if even a dozen have been killed this century. I heard of one man who came upon one eating on a moose near Stewart. He had a most extraordinary escape from death. The bear turned and charged. The man was unaccustomed to the bolt action of the rifle he was carrying and fumbled with the loading. He managed to get a cartridge into the chamber. Without having time to aim, he fired at the bear from the waist.

"The bullet struck the bear in the chest through the heart, but the bear's momentum kept the animal going. With one swipe of its claws the dead bear ripped the man's scalp off. He lost consciousness immediately.

"When the man came to, he found his head in the bear's mouth. He did not realize at first what was clamped over his head. Putting his hands up, he felt the bear's jaws. *Rigor mortis* had not set in so he managed to force the jaws apart enough to free himself. He placed his dangling scalp back over his head as best he could and wrapped his shirt around it. He reached a roadhouse just as a stagecoach was leaving for Whitehorse.

"That man survived and when I met him a year later, he had a scar completely around his head. He wore long hair to cover it. We remarked how lucky he was to have lived since a bear's jaws normally clamp shut as it dies.

"There is no recorded case of a northern wolf ever having attacked a human. Still, it is not wise to venture far from your cabin in the winter dusk.

"Wolves frequently came close to our cabin in Eagle Rock. Sometimes I could see their eyes glowing outside the window. If the door was opened and a light shone on them, they would slink away. The bolder ones would pad around the clearing surrounding the cabins on the lookout for dogs. Wolves never miss an opportunity to eat a dog. They have been known to snatch pups off the doorsills of cabins. They have even carried off some of our own full-grown huskies from Eagle Rock.

"In the spring of 1902 my uncles Fred and Frank Mack were driving a wagon. Sitting on the back seat of the wagon was Shep, a dog they had brought from Minneapolis across the Chilkoot Pass in 1898. They came to a place where there was deep brush on all sides. An albino timber wolf jumped out, grabbed the 60-pound Shep, and ran off into the bush.

"The men did not carry rifles to work, but they did have double-bitted axes. Fred went in after the animals and in a few feet found Shep dead with his throat torn open. The wolf was snarling over him. Fred swung the axe and split the wolf's head open. We had the pelt of that wolf. It had several tears in the back of the head.

"No human has ever been attacked by wolves in the Yukon to my knowledge, but there always remains the uncomfortable feeling that a pack of wolves might attack before realizing their victim's scent wasn't that of another animal.

"An Indian told us the following story. He was crossing the frozen Nisling Lake pulling a small sled when he heard wolves baying to gather for a kill. Their low cries and wails carried for miles, echoing in the hills. The Indian had nearly reached the opposite shore when he looked back. He saw a large pack of wolves trailing him. They were silent and had dropped into the killing lope, heads high, tails straight out. Some caribou had crossed the lake leaving their scent behind. This worried the Indian.

"He kept looking back. The wolves came steadily on at a slow lope aimed at wearing down a moose or caribou. He started running and made it safely up a poplar tree. There he waited until the wolves passed.

"Many animals grow to a large size in the north provided nature is not upset by human depredation or forest fires. Survival of the fittest applies. Wolves, lynx, and foxes all eat the weaker brethren of their own kind when food is in short supply.

"Some of the Yukon wolves are monsters in size, weighing 175 pounds or more. On one occasion I measured some wolf tracks with an ordinary enamel saucer. The saucer would not cover the larger tracks.

"These huge wolves are rarely caught. They are too canny. A trapper named George McDade once shot a wolf weighing more than 200 pounds near Yukon Crossing in 1925. It was so big and heavy that his sled had to be tipped on its side and the body eased on. The pelt measured eight feet in length.

"Among the most dangerous animals are bull moose during rut. Rut can put a normally docile moose in an ugly mood. They resent light at night. They have been known to charge lights from cars and trains.

"When two moose attack each other you can hear the terrible noise from their antlers at a great distance. These antlers are so hard, they could chip a steel axe blade.

"The only thing that a wolverine has to fear is the slow, ambling porcupine. In attacking the porcupine, they'll charge from the side trying to tip their meal on its back. The wolverine makes a quick grab to rip open the porcupine's stomach but usually gets a lashing from the green tail quills.

"Quills are barbed and can inflict terrible injuries on wolverines or dogs, especially to the head, nose, and inside the mouth. Animals go mad with pain as these quills work deeper into the flesh. There is always the danger that they'll work into the brain or an artery. That can be fatal. It is difficult to pull the quills out since the barbs slant backwards. They can work themselves out naturally.

"After killing the porcupine a wolverine will eat the meat cleanly, leaving only skin and quills. Man also eats porcupines. Many a freezing, starving trapper's life has been saved by the meat of these slow creatures.

"Still, man remains the most dangerous animal of the north."

Our children are leaving the bush to work in the cities of bright lights. They come back discouraged with life's ups and downs. Then they leave again, never to return."

Andrew Isaac

DOT LAKE, ALASKA

ANDREW ISAAC IS THE TRADITIONAL TRIBAL CHIEF OF
*the Athapaskan natives in the Tanana Valley of Alaska. He
was born in 1898, long before the housing development he lives
in on Dot Lake existed. Long before polyester clothes replaced
deerskins. Long before the land was sold and became private
property.*

*Isaac says the Alcan Highway signalled the end of old
Alaska. "It brought the white man in," he says. "We Indians
began to lose our aboriginal rights to the land, our hunting
rights, our culture. . . . I am fighting for my younger generations. They are the future of the Indian."*

"I'M THE TRADITIONAL CHIEF OF THE ENTIRE TANANA Valley Athapaskan tribe in central Alaska. I'm the guy. I living a long time. I understand. Therefore I'm talking for my native people and my young generations.

"Indians always here. Russians came in after and sold land to America. Then Alaska was a territory. I remember when the United States put up Alaska boundaries. I didn't understand what a boundary was; it wasn't the Indian way of life.

"We were born here. This was Indian land. We followed the caribou and moose during hunts. We didn't need papers or permits; there were no boundaries.

"Us Athapaskans grew up with cooperation. We helped each other. We lived under the Chief in harmony. We wore skin clothes, traded, and shared food. There was always enough meat. No hard times. No alcohol.

"After the white man came from the South 48 to prospect gold in Chicken, Dawson, O'Brien, Steel Creek, Eagle, Fairbanks, and Nome, they dug up the land and took the gold away. Indians not know the value of gold and show the white man where to find it. The white man filed claims. No thanks to the Indians.

"In 1915 the United States forms a reservation for us Indians. We didn't know what a reservation was. White ministers did the talking for us. We shut up and lost our land. We were never paid for it.

"In 1932 old Chief Peter asks for title to the land. We

didn't get title, but we could hunt and fish. Still, without title we can't cut timber, mine, or lease our land. Our land was swindled from us.

"All kinds of people then come in on our land to homestead. Our land became United States federal lands. Soon everybody has a license to hunt, and the game gets wiped out. The white man comes in with airplanes and shoots for sport. He wastes the meat. The moose season is limited to 10 days, and the whites kill off all the quotas. There's no moose left for the Indians. An oil pipeline gets put in, and the caribou no longer migrate to us.

"With the white man comes disease that kills the Indians, and alcohol. Indians can't tolerate alcohol. They go crazy. For a while there was a law that whites couldn't sell whiskey to the Indians. Every time an Indian got drunk, somebody died. If the seller was caught, he'd be fined and jailed for six months.

"Now the alcohol law is gone. Indians get drunk, freeze to death, kill, and commit suicide. Many go on white man's welfare. Our girls marry white men, and then the whites go back to South 48 and marry again. The girls go on welfare.

"All because us Indians not know what boundaries were to keep the whites out. Now I tell my young generations to get educations and good jobs so they can fight back for the land. Our land. I stay home now. I fight for my young generations."

just jammed the gun barrel down the hole and pulled the trigger. Got that wolverine, but the gun still has its teeth marks on it.

"Wolverine jaws are strong. They're the only animals who make a meal of moose antlers. They can snap a two-inch-thick stick in half. See that pelt on the wall? I had set a Number Two trap with hopes of catchin' a female lynx to breed and got that wolverine instead. See how his left toe is off? He was frothin' at the mouth and tearin' around in that trap. When I got there he was almost free and would have come for me.

"I didn't have a gun with me, but I did have a snare in my pack. I looked around quick and saw a stick. I tied on the snare, put it around his head, and gave it a jerk. Snapped off his toe, but I had him. Pure devil on a stick. That bugger was *this* close from my hands. Every time he grabbed that stick, he took splinters out. He weighed 41 pounds. It was all I could do to hold him. He was after me the whole time, and I had to keep backing around. Finally I got a hatchet out of my pack, let loose with one hand, and cracked his skull. A female lynx would have been a lot easier.

"Game used to be thick on the Kenai Peninsula. I was once guiding a crew through the mountains of Resurrection Pass. We got down to a clearing with some dead, scattered trees. There we counted 44 moose in one herd. The old bulls were grunting. It was during rut, and they was fightin' over the cows. Some of 'em got tangled in each other's antlers. I used to find carcasses with the antlers locked in a death struggle. Them moose starved to death. Probably died thinking about their sins.

"When the wolves came out in packs, the moose were hard to shoot. Those wolves single out weak moose and

caribou who lag behind the herds. They're the first to go. Those wolves can kill a caribou twice their length.

"Two years ago they killed a moose just down the hill from our house. All that was left by morning was a piece of skull in the crusty snow and a leg bone. I heard of one man who was treed by wolves in the winter of 1930. All they found was part of his clothes, the heels of his shoes, and empty .22 shells by the gun under the tree. They figured that the wolves must have been starving. He climbed this tree, emptied his gun, froze, and fell out. Those wolves also ate the wolves he killed, his clothes, and his bones.

"We used to see caribou all the time in Alaska during the 1930s. The herds back then were immense. One spring I saw a line of caribou that came across Resurrection Pass to Tetlin Lake that never broke for three days and nights. Just a solid river of deer, maybe 90,000 strong. I could look clear to the mountains from the lake and see that line, like a pencil mark, cutting right across the land.

"That's when I found out that the local Athapaskan Indians weren't such great conservationists. They were out there with .22s and .30/06s, just bangin' into that herd. For five miles Tetlin Lake looked like a slaughter house on the ice. The caribou that weren't killed staggered off.

"The herd finally veered right through town. Those Indians was between there and the trading post, buying up ammunition and blasting away. You could hear them old caribou moanin' in town. The place smelled of blood.

"You know, what them Indians liked best was the un-born calves from the cows in spring. Old John used to tell me, 'Boy caribou—him good.' That's the tenderest meat, I guess.

"Them caribou are gutsy buggers. I was once hunting

one winter on crusty snow. Heavy animals were breaking through, and it slowed them up. Well, I shot this caribou who was almost out of range. The bullet cut both front legs off below the knees. He disappeared over the hill!

"I took that bugger's trail and followed him for two miles. The snow was red; you'd think there was enough blood in him for 20 caribou. When I caught up with him he was running, and the skin was peeled back. He was just poking bone stubs across the snow. Them buggers have some endurance."

Seymour Abel

EAGLE, ALASKA

SEYMOUR ABEL AND JAN WALDRON, HIS COMMON-
law wife, live off the bounty of the land with their young son,
Leif Beaudine. They are part of a community of river people,
docked in houseboats in a remote slough of the Yukon River.

The Abels and their friends hide from the Bureau of Land
Management, which hunts for squatters on federal land. They
pay no taxes and keep no social security cards, driver's licenses,
mortgages, credit cards, or bank accounts. No benefits are
expected from the society they quit. They shoot game to eat.
Clothes are fashioned from animal skins. Every few months, the
Abels come into the outpost town of Eagle to barter for supplies at
a food cooperative.

The Abels subsist outside the law but do not consider them-
selves outlaws. Their lifestyle is a personal protest against a
society with which they are disenchanted. "Live and let live,"

they say. It is understood that emergencies must be solved on their own, or they will perish in the wilderness.

"We're living the way our ancestors did on the frontier," Seymour Abel says. "It's been the traditional American way for hundreds of years. In a real democracy, you'd be free to do this. But in America, you have to live the way they tell you. . . . We'll hold out like this as long as we can—or until something else comes along."

"I LEFT TENNESSEE TO HOMESTEAD IN ALASKA, BUT THE Feds ended the Homesteading Act in 1971 just as I arrived. I ended up building a cabin with a friend near Delta Junction and living off food stamps. Soon Delta Junction got too crowded with Cadillac homesteaders living in their Winnebagos and slinging guns like John Wayne. I moved on.

"In 1975 I met Jan Waldron. We left Anchorage to live a subsistence life on our own. We built a riverboat on the Yukon River and took it 70 miles down the river past Eagle. We anchored in a slough, stove up the boat, and constructed a make-shift cabin out of the wood, an old army tent liner, and styrofoam. We stayed for two years and became friendly with other river people living on what was federal land.

"We'd come into town by canoe or dog sled about five times a year to get mail and staple supplies. We practically lived on the game we shot: beavers, moose, bear, caribou, ducks, and muskrats. We also learned how to make a fish wheel and caught up to 60 pounds of King salmon a season.

We made our clothes from caribou pelts. There is no shortage of game out in the bush; we believe that the Fish and Game Department permits and regulations really apply to the urban areas like Anchorage and Fairbanks where you have denser populations of hunters. It hurts to regulate the bush using urban standards.

"It cost us an average of $2,000 a year to outfit me, Jan, and our young son, Leif Beaudine. That comes to $1,200 for food and $800 for hardware. We joined a food coop in Eagle that imports organically grown food from Seattle. We'd get 50 pounds of buckwheat and whole grain flour for $11; 50 pounds of corn for $6.50; 25 pounds of brown rice for $7.25; 50 pounds of rye for $8; 200 pounds of wheat for $30; 100 pounds of oats for $20; 40 pounds of peanut butter for $50; 10 gallons of safflower oil for $50; two gallons of soy sauce for $11; 20 pounds of noodles for $11; and about 150 pounds of dried raisins, nuts, dates, figs, and fruit. It was difficult to ship it all downriver to our hiding place in canoes, but we did it.

"We don't waste anything. When we shoot a moose we break open the bones for marrow, make clothes from the pelt, and take all them guts and clean them out. We even clean yards of squiggly intestines and make beaudine out of it. Beaudine means 'good eating' in French. Stuffed with sausage, moose meat, squash, and onions, it's good eating! Fat and greasy. Our son liked it so much, we found a name for him.

"We're pretty self-sufficient out there. I will never rely on food stamps or welfare again. It may be feast or famine in the bush, but it's better than getting trapped into the government machine or paying taxes for a system we don't ethically support.

"We make our own toboggans and dog sleds, raise our own puppies, make shoes out of hide leather, and pay for our food with pelts we skin out.

"Our senses have become heightened out here. Your life can be in danger when things go wrong. So you're more aware. When we get sick, we have to heal ourselves naturally. If we get really sick, we die. That's an accepted fact of life out here.

"We go for long spells without seeing other people, but when we do see friends, the meetings are more meaningful. We've become more instinctive and perceptive now that we're away from crowds. It's more satisfying to rely on yourself and make it. I've really refined my skills.

"Things are starting to change. In a way, now that public land is no longer really public, and the Bureau of Land Management is burning down bush cabins on federal land, we've become fugitives from the law. Fugitives from society. Between the state and federal lands and the Native Land Claim Settlement, everything is owned. Even if people never come near the land. It's a shame 'cause the river people don't bother anybody. Society just hates to know that we exist outside the law."

Jack Boone

EAGLE, ALASKA

JACK BOONE IS A DESCENDANT OF DANIEL BOONE AND *also espouses "that old frontier individualism." He left California to homestead in Juneau. When that became too crowded for him he packed up his family and drove to Eagle at the northern end of the Taylor Highway. There he built an octagonal cabin flush against the woods of the Yukon-Charley wilderness.*

Boone is a bearish man with a sonorous voice. He honed his fishing and hunting skills and became a self-proclaimed "conservationist." Conservation, in Boone's vision, includes not only animals in the wild, "but a man chasing those animals." He deplores "effete" environmental organizations such as the Sierra Club. Bumper stickers on his pickup truck include: "Sierra Go Home," "Eat Moose—10,000 Wolves Can't All Be Wrong," and "Protect Bears—They Eat Environmentalists."

Boone advocates stewardship of the land. He led a group of

Eagle residents in vocal protests against the federal government when the Carter Administration tried to "lock up" the Yukon-Charley territory into a national monument. He testified in Congress against proposed land legislation. As a last resort, he proclaims the right of civil disobedience, including violence.

"People who can hunt, trap, fish, and subsist in the woods are few in number," Boone says. "They are the real endangered species."

"All of a sudden all these conservationists are coming out of the woodwork to tell us how to save Alaska."

—TED STEVENS

"The history of liberty is the history of resistance . . . it is a history of the limitation of governmental power."

—WOODROW WILSON

"Liberty too can corrupt, and absolute liberty can corrupt absolutely."

—GERTRUDE HIMMELFARB

"Leave me alone."   —JACK BOONE

"I CAME INTO THE COUNTRY IN 1974 WITH A WIFE AND four kids to escape the tyranny of South 48 regulations. I've only been out of Alaska 24 hours since I came here. We like our simple subsistence lifestyle here and feel that it is all threatened by encroaching federal legislation to make this area into a wilderness monument.

"See, it's this old Alaska individualism—a guy goin' out into the bush and doing what he feels like doing. This is one of the last frontiers on this over-populated earth where individuals have the freedom to act as they please. We come to live here because we like our personal freedom. We feel that it is our right as Americans.

"What we're talking about is an endangered way of life. We read all about the list of endangered species. We all have an understanding in the back of our minds of why we don't want to see the last whale or peregrine falcon die. Still, their advantage to mankind is hard to put a cash value on. I'll get along just as well without the peregrine falcon. But just the same, I don't want it to disappear.

"When the last guy that can walk out into the bush with nothing but a pack on his back and survive goes, mankind will have lost something a lot more serious than a peregrine falcon. There's very few of us left who can go out into the woods, build a cabin, trap, hunt, fish, and make it. All-around woodsmen. And yet, we're the only endangered species that can still be hunted by Bureau of Land Management helicopters and run out of the country. We're being legis-

lated out of existence by thousands of rules thought up in Washington, D.C. that say, 'You can't do this any more.'

"This isn't going to be the same place when the trails are all marked by the National Park Service and there are 'Camp Here' signs everywhere. You're trading an awful lot when you give up the right to go out and shoot a moose for *permission* to do the same thing. We don't want to live in an area where you can't breathe without a permit.

"Now, I can understand the need to regulate the huge oil and mineral companies and their relationship to the land. They have a greater impact on the environment than us subsistence people living and sacrificing on $1,000 a year. Compared to them, we're 'bush league.' We can't hire expensive lawyers to fight legislation the way they do.

"It's ironic that subsistence people in Eagle are being regulated. We're the real conservationists. We don't use up a lot of the earth's resources. We don't pollute our environment. We don't overpopulate the area and, in a place where winter temperatures plummet to minus 70 degrees, there is no rush of people waiting to move in. We have even come to realize that Eagle has to stay primitive to keep things in balance. We voted down putting in extensive telephone, electrical, and sewage services. We have no desire to pave the Taylor Highway that leads into town. We don't need any more regulation.

"The other irony is that whenever the Park Service moves in, they develop the very areas they posture to preserve. They build roads into the parks, tourist facilities, and park headquarters. They bring in rangers making $40,000 a year and promote unknown areas to bring in more tourists.

"In the 'wilderness' areas, the Feds lock up lands and call it 'natural.' Well, it's not natural. It's an artificial zoo

environment. The natural ecosystem has always involved a moose with a man chasing it. If there were no men, the moose would over-multiply and die of starvation.

"It's a question of freedom out here. We don't want to live in a police state. People in Eagle are quiet, law-abiding, and pacifistic, but we'll fight for our rights if backed up against a wall, monument, or national park. Patrick Henry did not say, 'Give me liberty, or give me a better compromise with the King.' If we have to, we'll die for the right *not* to be governed by people who make decisions for us 3,000 miles away."

Frank Betts

McKinley National Park, Alaska

Frank Betts is the Superintendent of McKinley *National Park—a vast treasure dwarfed within Alaska's 586,400 square miles of land. He is employed by the Department of the Interior, and his paycheck comes from an office in Washington, D.C. This, together with a "Save Alaska From the Alaskans" philosophy, infuriates people who came north to get away from federal regulation.*

Betts defends the national park system in an era of massive land exploitation and development. He responds, indirectly, to people like Jack Boone.

"Land? Well, they aren't making any more of it."

—WILL ROGERS

"I'M THE PARK SUPERINTENDENT OF MCKINLEY National Park. I know that there's a lot of talk about the federal government locking up federal lands owned by the public. A lot of Alaskans resent this because it interferes with their former lifestyles. Still, public lands are owned by the public. That includes Americans in the South 48. When the majority votes to preserve these lands, that's democracy. Until we change the democratic system that's the way we pass legislation.

"It comes down to save Alaska from the Alaskans. We put in regulations which allow people to use and enjoy the land and to protect land and wildlife. Each national monument is unique in some way. We seek to preserve these wilderness areas for us, for our children, and for future generations. There was no threat to Yellowstone National Park when it was created in 1872. People thought the idea was folly then. But look at the area around the place now. I feel better knowing that *some* land is protected in parks from South 48 developers and from 400,000 Alaskans.

"As to the fear that the Feds will let subsistence people and pioneers die a death of attrition, that's not true. We are issuing grandfather permits to people who can prove that they lived subsistence lifestyles on lands before they were

withdrawn from entry in 1972. The land has not been locked
up from their use.

"Still, we don't want people from Anchorage and Fairbanks claiming that they're subsistence people with a right
to build cabins wherever they wish. Nobody really subsists
anymore. Maybe the word should be 'supplement.' We all
use society to some degree to buy clothes, food, and fuel.

"In sum, many Alaskans resent the park service and
anybody who tells them that they can't always get their own
way, right or wrong."

Jean Keith Murray

KENNY LAKE, ALASKA

JEAN KEITH MURRAY IS A HOMESTEADER LIVING IN *Kenny Lake. The view outside his cabin is of the Wrangell Mountain Range. His nearest neighbor lives 15 miles away.*

Getting land to homestead in the 1970s was fraught with red tape and obstacles, Murray said. It took years of effort in California to get his "40 acres and a mule" under provisions enacted by the Homestead Act of 1840.

Once Murray got his land, he built a wooden teepee and heated it with a woodburning stove. That would get him through the first winter while he built his insulated one-room cabin.

"Land is power. The federal government is loathe to part with either," Murray said in a gentle voice. "That's why us homesteaders had such problems getting what, after all, was supposed to be public land. Perhaps the Feds were testing to see how serious we were. But I think it was a fundamental reluctance to

116

part with the land. People in government have become civil masters instead of civil servants."

As Murray speaks, he prepares a subsistence meal—grouse, shaggy mane mushrooms plucked from the front yard, bull moose flank steak, and an "appetizer" of moose testicles. The remains of the moose were donated by a friend and lay spread out by the original teepee, which is now inhabited by his goats. The hide would be left to dry in the sun.

Murray is one of relatively few homesteaders who pulled through the Alaska land claim process in the 1970s. He promises to give the homestead to his grandson as a trust, but now must contend with a sizable inheritance tax.

"There's always some obstacle the government drops in your way," he said. "But I never expected it would be easy."

"MOST PEOPLE LIKE ME HAVE MOVED INTO THE Alaskan bush to avoid conforming. Nonconformance deprives big government of some of its power. The system tries to make you want to conform. You're brainwashed subtly into being a 'citizen.' The more you conform, the more you lose control.

"The federal government owns two-thirds of Alaskan lands, a hangover from territorial days. In this way the Feds are landlords. The only power a landlord has over its tenants is the land it owns. To keep us in control, the 1862 Homesteading Act has new restrictions and regulations that make it even more difficult to acquire land.

"Some government tricks played on homesteaders during this century were to offer swamps, mountain tops, and land without road access to applicants in the South 48. They'd list this land to satisfy the letter of the Homesteading Act. Now the Bureau of Land Management is trying to get rid of squatters and homesteaders by declaring federal lands 'monuments.' You can't trespass or develop monuments in any way. You can't even *fly* over them. This is in the name of preserving wilderness. Or, to increase the tax base, federal lands are going to tycoons and boomers in the oil and mineral industries. *They* get the land. Not to mention federal lands used by the military that equal the acreage of Massachusetts.

"It took me seven years to get a piece of land to homestead from the time I made my application as a contractor in Los Angeles until the time my application was processed. If the government really wanted to give away land, would it have taken that long?

"I applied for land at age 51. I wanted to live a subsistence lifestyle and to eventually pass the land on to my son as a trust. First I had to convince the Department of the Interior that I was a viable candidate. The requirements were simple but specific, and the government had a system that stacked the odds against you.

"The government had several tactics in turning applicants down. If one asked, 'Is any land available?' he'd be told, 'No place is open.' Catch-22. If the applicant was asked, 'Where do you want to homestead?' and replied, 'I don't care where,' he'd be told that there was a freeze on federal land until the native land claims were settled. Catch-22.

118

"If an applicant was too specific, and asked the government for particular lots on particular quadrants of land, he might be told the land was taken. Catch-22.

"The government also told homestead applicants that land was available, but that it would cost them money. They'd have to hire bulldozers to clear their acreage, find the time and funds to build a cabin, and remain on their land steadily for over five years. Homesteaders, almost by definition, lack sufficient funds. Catch-22.

"Homesteaders were restricted by the government to acquiring no more than 160 acres of land. To meet the requirement of cultivating 20 acres, one needs irrigation. Sometimes this is not possible when you only have 160 acres or less. Catch-22.

"Many get through the homesteading application process only to leave during the Alaskan winter because they don't have time to build shelter. Their land is confiscated. Catch-22.

"Only one percent of all applicants succeed in acquiring land from the government. To get through the winter I built a huge wooden teepee in a week that I could heat with a wood stove. *Then* I built my cabin. I filed for 160 acres and got 80. Now the government is trying to tax me off my land. Catch-22."

Yule Kilcher

HOMER, ALASKA

HOMER IS A TOWN THAT RESTS ON A SPIT OF SAND AT *the tip of the Kenai Peninsula. It overlooks Kachemak Bay and a range of dormant volcanoes, some rising from the sea on their own islands, others connected by glacial couloirs.*

Yule Kilcher came to Homer from Switzerland to scout for land before the outbreak of World War II. He was part of a group of young, avant-garde Europeans who saw war approaching. They wanted to homestead a better life.

While Kilcher was away, his friends were inducted and killed in the War. One woman survived. She took a steamer to America, married Kilcher, and returned with him to Alaska.

Kilcher champions self-reliance. He keeps chickens, gardens, and runs a modest potato farm. His house, barn, and meditation yurt are surrounded by acres of meadows and spruce. The fragrance of pine resin and wood smoke hangs in the air. Kilcher collects coal that gathers on his beach and burns it in the stove for heat.

Kilcher is a survivalist who is fearful of the "inevitable" collapse of civilization and World War III. He believes that rural Alaska, at a remove from urban centers, will provide a buffer zone in hard times to come.

"The human race's prospects of survival were considerably better when we were defenseless against tigers than they are today when we have become defenseless against ourselves."

—ARNOLD TOYNBEE

"I AM A SURVIVALIST. I WAS BORN IN SWITZERLAND. I joined an avant-garde group of young people including Germans and Austrians. We wanted to homestead and were willing to take the big step of turning our backs on civilization. At the time, World War II was brewing. I had met Hitler in a beer hall. I wasn't impressed. I could see the trump, trump, trump sort of progress he was creating. I saw war coming then. I see war coming now.

"I learned that in unfavorable circumstances the human community regresses easily into barbarity. Civilizations col-

lapse at the core first. It's people living on the fringes who survive longer.

"My avant-garde friends and I decided that we wanted land where there were fruit trees but far enough north so that we would be out of harm's way should war break out. We drew a latitude line across the northern hemisphere. It took in Norway, Siberia, Alaska, and the Canadian Northwest Territories.

"I was chosen as the scout. I decided first to look for land in Alaska. Just before World War II broke out, I left Europe on the steamer *Rex.* I hitched across America from New York to Prince Rupert, Canada. I stowed away on a ship bound up the inland fiords to Seward, Alaska.

"Well, upon reaching Seward I met a friend who told me that I could get to a place named Homer by walking across the Harding ice fields and Kenai Mountains. It was an adventure which I decided to try. I was only 23 and inexperienced. I took off with no maps or anything.

"After about five days on the ice fields, I ran into snow and rain. I turned back to Seward to take another route to Homer. I followed the railroad tracks west to Cooper Landing. From there I followed a sled dog trail through the swamps.

"There I met a Swede named Anderson. He was a well-known guide, naturalist, and trapper who knew the area. He lived on an island in Skilak Lake and invited me to his house. 'Follow the sled dog trail,' he said, 'and travel west with the sun until you hit the lake. It's on the way to Homer.' He warned me not to raft across the lake because of sudden squalls and then struck off, following his traplines.

"On the way to Skilak Lake, I met my first brown bear. It was scary. The sun was out after a heavy rain. Everything was wet. The grass was about six feet tall in front of me, and I was sauntering along. I had taken an old-timer's advice to have a frying pan ready to hit to scare bears away.

"So I was walking along when all of a sudden, I think about my native Bern, Switzerland. It's the capital, and a bear is part of the city's coat of arms. They have a zoo in the center of town with a big bear pit in it, and it smells.

"All of a sudden I wonder, 'Why do you think about all of that?' And I realize that I smell bear.

"I stopped right there, looked around, and didn't see anything. So I took my frying pan and made a hell of a noise with my gun barrel. Scared shitless, you know? Then, 50 feet ahead of me, I see the grass move. I banged the pan some more, waited 10 minutes, and advanced some more.

"I came across some bear tracks as big as a hat. The swamp water was still seeping into them. I was glad he ran away. I smelled him first. It's funny how the subconscious works.

"That same day I met Nutter — Alaska's foremost trapper of wolves. I came upon his cabin and hollered, 'Anybody home?' I could see smoke coming out of the chimney.

"Well, this big giant of a man jumps out of that cabin, split ass naked. He growls in a deep booming voice, 'Who's there?' Unshaven, real caveman type, you know? He had been taking a bath. He turned out to be very well-educated. Gave me a fine supper and lots of advice. He also gave me directions towards Skilak Lake. Very nice.

"Finally I come to Skilak Lake. I had brought a few railroad spikes with me, wire, rope, and a good hatchet. I was a very good axeman from lumbering days in Sweden. I stripped, jumped into the lake, and fetched three sturdy driftwood logs. It was a cold glacial lake. The warm July weather heated the top 16 inches of water, so I kept my knees up and swam on the surface as best I could.

"Once ashore I bullnosed the logs, giving them a canoe-bow profile. I fashioned crosspieces and lashed everything together. Then I whittled a paddle out of a straight stick of spruce. Disregarding Anderson's advice, I put my pack, clothes, and gun on top of the raft and paddled off. I kept my logging boots on and strapped on corks to help keep me afloat in case I fell off.

"I thought I could easily cross that four mile lake. The raft was 30 feet long and pretty solid. I paddled five strokes on the left, five strokes on the right. Very nice.

"Then, about half way across, the lake started to ripple. Fifteen minutes later the ripples turned to wavelets, and the wavelets turned to foot-high waves. The wind came up, and with it a squall.

"I lost headway as I passed a waterfall coming down off a glacier on shore. I was within a mile of the other shore when the waves became two feet high. I had to paddle like hell on one side to keep the raft from turning upstream. Soon there was a blister on my thigh. I got tired from paddling on one side, so I tried to paddle backwards over my other side. Then, the raft started to break apart.

"One log almost came free, so I took my hatchet and drove the spike in better. By the time I did that I was headed back upstream toward the head of the glacier. I paddled like hell to get going in the right direction. This time the other side started to fall apart.

"Now, I had absolutely given up to be afraid. I had been in danger of losing my life so many times before. I have almost been blown down the mouth of Mount Vesuvius. I've fought typhoid fever. I have looked into the wrong ends of

Arab gun barrels while crossing the Sahara Desert. I have climbed the Matterhorn using a rain cape as a sail to keep moving before night. Danger just wasn't worth worrying about. No time to be afraid, you know? At the time it was just a challenge to see *how* the hell I was going to get out of another bad situation.

"So I lashed the raft together again and pressed on into choppy waves three feet high. Soon everything was coming apart. The water was churned up, and I was all icy wet. I headed towards a promontory with the waves splashing up against it and saw a gap about 20 feet wide. I paddled for that.

"Through this gap in the rocks was a tiny lagoon, 100 feet across with a 40 foot beach. The raft came to a peaceful landing. No wind. No waves. Just calm and serene in there. All I had on were my boots. Holding my gun I walked up to a little ridge. There was a cow moose and two calves standing there. They looked at me and walked off. Real peaceful after this ordeal.

"I returned to the beach and built a fire. I gathered some mushrooms, cranberries, and killed a spruce grouse for dinner. I fell asleep to the sound of the wind and storm raging outside the lagoon.

"By morning the wind had abated. I took the raft outside and made a sail out of my rain cape. I paddled down the lake for 10 miles with the help of a breeze coming down off the glacier.

"It was beautiful. I was sailing along with no clothes on, singing at the top of my lungs. It was my world and I was feeling great. I was so elated and happy that morning that I didn't even hear the sound of an outboard motor until it came around the corner. It was Anderson and his wife. He had heard singing and told his wife to turn the radio off. There I was.

"I quickly put on my pants, kicked the raft goodbye and went along to their island. We landed at a pier. There were geese swimming around and 10-foot-high dahlias on shore. I stayed with the Andersons all day and then got directions to Tustumena Lake and Homer.

"The next day I crossed a swamp. There were just a few small spruce stumps left standing. I waded through. I was almost out when this huge bull moose with a massive rack comes by leading several cows and calves. They must have been a reception committee.

"Now, I was still a Swiss greenhorn. Seeing these animals was new to me. I foolishly hid behind an eight-foot-high spruce stump. The trunk was three inches across. Any child could knock it over.

"These moose—they started to advance towards me. Curious, you know? They stopped about 150 yards from my nose. Then they started to advance again.

"I had a harmonica in my rucksack. I took it out and started to play. And these moose—they all stop. They cocked their big heads and listened with big ears. When I stopped playing, they'd come closer very carefully to investigate. I'd play again and they stop again.

"Finally I had all the moose standing in a semicircle around me within 50 feet, listening to my concert. I was very honored. Funny as hell.

"This went on for a while, but soon I had to go. They were waiting for an encore but enough was enough. I went 'SHOO.' They shooed for 20 feet and then peered back at me. I'd shoo some more. They'd retreat some more. I screwed my courage and banged my gun barrel on the frying pan and then walked right through these moose and out of the swamp.

"Eventually I reached Tustumena Lake where a fisherman picked me up in his skiff. Reaching Homer I looked around, liked what I saw, and prepared to return to Europe to tell my friends. They were all dead when I returned— killed in the war except for one woman. I married her off the boat and returned with her to Homer to live. There we built this cabin, grew our own food, fished, and survived.

"I am collecting survival knowledge here. I have contacted some valuable people through my friend Paul Petzoldt, the founder of the National Outdoor Leadership School. I have access to craftsmen with skills including blacksmithing, brickmaking, and woodworking. They could come here if things ever turned bad. We could survive.

"I have a story that I tell my liberal friends when they visit. If I were on an excursion boat in the South Pacific and got wrecked, I'd immediately find a lifeboat. If I had a choice of rowing to shore with a bunch of rednecks or with a bunch of Eastern Establishmentarians, I'd go with the rednecks. The Eastern liberals would get ashore and immediately form committees. They'd work by consensus, debate endlessly, and they wouldn't know how to dig a clam. Nothing would get done. They'd starve to death. The rednecks are survivors. They might try to kill each other, but they'd know how to survive.

"Civilizations are like soap bubbles. They're precarious. The prettiest ones are the thin ones with beautiful colors. They burst first. Civilizations arise in the terminal stages of social development. Every civilization thinks that *it's* going to make it, just like every war is the 'last' war. This is a delusion, the prelude to a gradual, unspectacular grinding down. Everything will crumble in a domino effect some day.

"People are dependent on society and civilization. When the rules break down, and people begin to starve, you find that they're no longer so civilized. Hunger leads to civil unrest. You find the hordes of urban dwellers descend on the countryside to rob and pillage. It could happen if we don't develop a stronger spiritual base to balance out our technological strength and defense. I'll be prepared."

B. J. Solomon

CHITINA, ALASKA

B. J. SOLOMON WAS A DIVORCED GRANDMOTHER WHEN *she decided Los Angeles had become too crowded and polluted. She pulled up her stakes and hitchhiked to Alaska. She didn't settle in Fairbanks or Anchorage but in Chitina, a remote outpost surrounded by the Wrangell Mountains.*

Chitina was a waystation in the 1920s for a train that carried miners to the Kennecott Copper operation in McCarthy. A few diehards remain in Chitina today, long after the close of the mining operation.

As a joke, one resident painted ghosts on the walls of a Chitina barn. He etched ghosts into the windows of Rita Hatch's Bar. Ghosts turn up in graffiti at the Skid Row gas station. Locals insist the town isn't a ghost town. Just quiet.

But not quiet enough for Solomon. She took up quarters in an abandoned trapper's cabin five miles outside town on a bluff overlooking the Copper River. There she started life anew, venturing into town only to pick up mail dropped by the weekly mail plane or to talk when she needs a friend.

"For 22 years as a suburban housewife in Los Angeles I dreamed of leaving everything behind and coming to Alaska. Society almost trapped me until I got up the gumption to leave.

"I was living in a four-bedroom, two-story house. I passed my time stripping wax off the dining room floor, painting window sills, mowing the lawn, and keeping up with the Joneses. I rarely questioned a perceived obligation to do this sort of thing.

"Los Angeles turned into an obscenity since the time I grew up there. You get up into the mountains over the city and see all that black smog covering the sky. You start to feel personally responsible for its being there. Suburbia had become sterile and antiseptic to me. Its peace and solitude was contrived; the life it held out was dead and boring.

"In 1974 I left everything behind including a husband, my children, grandchildren, and all my possessions. I bought a van and traveled around the country. After living alone in Maine for a while my conscience started nagging me. 'B.J., you should be going to Alaska.' Finally that's what I did.

"The van was on its last legs in Idaho, and I sold it. I wrote 'Alaska' on a sign and began to hitchhike. It wasn't chores to keep me busy. I've been snowbound for up to six weeks straight. It's dark and cold, and I can feel cabin fever creeping in. I find myself talking to myself. Or looking over the bluff at the river and mountains, singing at the top of my lungs. But then, just as fast, I fall into deep depressions. Still, it's no worse than the depression and loneliness of the big cities.

"After weeks by yourself, going into Chitina becomes a culture shock. I go in for groceries and conversation and after 20 minutes find myself running home again. Living out here alone changes you.

"Some years ago I couldn't make it through the winter here. I bought a plane ticket back to Los Angeles. Well, the shock started as soon as I boarded the airplane. I felt herded onto the plane like cattle. When we landed I felt the magnetism of the city. I began to think of squirrels running nowhere in cages. You've got to go at everyone else's pace in the city, or you get rear-ended.

"Back in the South 48 it started to get really bad. I went to see some shrinks. They told me I was suffering from the start of a nervous breakdown. Soon they were shoving pills down my throat and appointments into their schedules. I began to understand that as soon as I got out of that city and back into the woods, I'd be all right. But wilderness wasn't a part of their mind set. They told me that going back would kill me. They gave me some more tranquilizers.

"Well, I listened to that inner voice again and left. After six months back in the cabin the woods cured me. Everything is back in order. Except sometimes I hear inner voices saying, 'It's time to go to Tibet.' When I hear that I feel insecure and head into town. But all in all I'm no longer a part of the lonely crowd. I'm much more in tune with myself out here. I feel that I've beaten the rat race and society."

Sally Gibert

McCarthy, Alaska

DURING THE ICE AGE, ANCIENT SNOWS CONDENSED *beneath their own weight and formed glaciers. Some of these icy massifs remain in Alaska today, including the Root and Kennicott glaciers which start high in Mount Blackburn and descend into a nameless valley.*

In summer, cataracts of meltwater thunder through turquoise ice caves. The glacial waters gather into the Nizina and Kennicott rivers. At their confluence is McCarthy, a has-been mining town.

The bridge leading to McCarthy washed away in a spring freshet. The town's score of year-round residents voted not to replace it. To get across the rivers, people must straddle a primitive wooden plank, suspended in mid-air by ropes and pulleys, and pull themselves.

Old Fords, Dodges, and John Deere tractors rust in over-

grown backyards. Heavy equipment only gets across when the rivers freeze. It's too much effort to remove it once it has outlived its usefulness.

McCarthy is a timepiece from the 1920s when miners came in on the train to work for Kennecott. When the company closed the mine, the train stopped running.

Today the windows of the stationhouse are boarded up. Weeds grow through its decayed floors. The turntable, poised in fulcral balance, can still be pushed in a squeeky arc but hasn't turned a train back to Chitina in more than 50 years.

The McCarthy Lounge stands in the center of town, its Victorian false front weathered with age. The Bear Den Saloon is annexed to the lounge. A hand-painted sign over the door reads: "Open most nights. Closed when slow." It's usually slow in McCarthy.

Sally Gibert lives in the General Merchandise Building, built in 1911. She came to Alaska from California and saved her money to buy and restore the building. She hopes to turn the place into a bed and breakfast hostel and talks about what it's like to live in McCarthy.

"WHEN YOU'RE LIVING AT THE END OF THE ROAD, IT takes some effort to get here. The tram and winter ice is the final buffer zone. Only those with a purpose arrive. The casual tourist is cut out.

"There is a smallness about McCarthy that is really comfortable and yet we're surrounded by such hugeness. We're preparing for small-scale existence in view of large-scale landscape. Winter can be very isolating for the 20 people who stick it out here. When the mail plane can't get through, you're really cut off from society. But then there are those in town who feel, 'We're not snowed in. The rest of the world is just snowed out.' They breathe a collective sigh of relief in winter.

"You get to know everyone in subtle ways here. Like Jerry's whistle. It's a real common sound. You know people by their whistles, footsteps, and mannerisms. You hear the muffled roar of the rivers, the rustling of aspen leaves, and the wind. You don't hear cars, horns, or jackhammers. Even the people who visit this place seem more quiet and respectful.

"I resent it when people call me 'Ghost Town Sally.' We're not ghosts, and there's a lot going on here now that wasn't going on back in the mining heydays. We're into New Age living. We're jacking up foundations and renovating buildings, like the General Merchandise Store I bought. I plan to turn it into a hostel. We'll serve Wrangell mud coffee and sourdough pancakes and live communally.

"My building was built in 1911 and was moved to this site in 1931. I'm still finding old relics like a bottle of 100 proof moonshine hidden behind a shelf. There's a cold-meat storage room with thin wooden boards lining the walls. We're also restoring the prostitute cabins out back, and the sauna.

"McCarthy may be isolated, but there is an alternative to cabin-fever winters in small-town Alaska. We're building a new way of life here on old foundations."

Joe Redington, Sr. and Sue Butcher

KNIK, ALASKA

SLED DOG RACES HAD THEIR ORIGINS IN THE YUKON *Gold Rush. Sourdoughs were gamblers and placed bets on which dog was strongest and fastest. Some events started with barroom bets like the fictional pulling contest in Jack London's "The Call of the Wild." During the Nome Stampede in 1908, a $10,000 winner-take-all sled race was held. This first formal race spread sporting fever far and wide.*

The granddaddy of all dog races is the Iditarod, organized in 1967 by Joe Redington, Sr., and Dorothy Page of Knik. The annual 1,050 mile race from Anchorage to Nome follows the sled route Leonard Seppala took in the winter of 1925 to carry serum to diphtheria victims. Fifty-nine sled teams and contestants from all over the world entered that first race, competing for

$25,000 to $50,000 awards.

Redington and Sue Butcher, his partner, have competed in the Iditarod and placed "in the money" several times. They met on a musk-ox farm in Unalaska. Redington was fishing, and Butcher was helping collect musk-ox fur for Inuit women to knit into clothing. They shared an interest in animals and decided to join forces to breed 150 dogs in Knik. When the wind blows in the right direction, the dogs' howls can be heard 10 miles away in Wasilla.

In 1979 Redington and Butcher decided to test a theory proposed by scientists from Yukon's North Arctic Institute that dogs could not survive high altitudes. The mushers selected seven of their best dogs and organized an expedition to climb 20,320-foot Mount McKinley.

Redington and Butcher were joined by Rob Stapleton, a photographer, and Ray Genêt, a guide. Genêt was the only one of the group to have "climbed a hill" before. (He later died on Mount Everest.)

Redington and Butcher talk about their adventure.

"IN RAISING CHAMPION RACING DOGS," BUTCHER SAID, "we try to breed the fastest, smartest, and toughest dogs we can. These dogs here are Alaskan huskies as opposed to Siberian huskies, Eskimo dogs, or malemutes. We have bred in hound, collie, Labrador, coyote, wolf, and fox to improve

strength, intelligence, and temperament.

"The breed has gotten better since the Fur Rendezvous races held in the 1920s. Back then champion dogs were loping at 15 miles per hour. Today we have dogs that trot at 14 miles per hour and lope at a steady 19 miles per hour. Our dogs are bred to run up to 18 hours and 100 miles a day, which is what we do for two weeks during the Iditarod competition.

"We train the dogs all through summer, dragging a sled behind them through the dirt in teams of eight. We run 'em anywhere from 20 to 60 miles a day, depending on the heat. They love to mush. They're happiest when on the trail.

"We also treat the dogs with love and kindness, and keep 'em free of parasites. Mushers who beat dogs don't win races."

"We feed them well on cattle scraps and salmon heads," Redington said. "Instead of throwing this nutritious food away, the dogs make use of it."

"Part of training a winning team is finding a natural leader. The leader controls the speed and sets the pace. A good leader will drop down to a pace he knows is comfortable for the other dogs," Butcher said. "He can't drag the team to Nome.

"A good lead dog has to take your commands. *Gee* means go right. *Haw* means go left. *Mush* can mean go forward or *hike*. I used to say, *Okay*, but that was dangerous. They may hear the word used in casual conversation on the trail and disappear over the horizon without you. *Whoa* is a good command for stop.

"Good lead dogs must also be able to locate the trail easily, even when it's covered with snow. Finding trails can increase your speed. This can save your life. One of my dogs

used her nose. Another felt for the packed trail under the snow with his feet.

"Some dogs have incredible memories. I was on a trail one year, and there was a log across it. We had to pull off into the woods to get around it. Well, one year later we were racing down that same hill, and all of a sudden the leader veered off into those woods. I had forgotten about that log, but she remembered."

"The Iditarod Race is relaxing compared to all of the preparation beforehand," Redington said. "Sponsors must invest an average of $5,000 for equipment and food. Once on the trail, you've got to get 20 food drops ready to pick up at 20 check points along the way.

"You must start with at least eight dogs and finish with at least five. You must take a 24-hour rest stop at one of the cabin check points along the way. It's a great feeling once you're under way. You don't see cars or other people from Anchorage to Nome. You sleep on your sled in a down sleeping bag, read no newspapers, forget all your troubles. You just race for 1,000 miles."

"In Alaska 1,000 miles takes you through all kinds of terrain," Butcher said. "Starting around Knik, there are flat hills, spruce and aspen forests. We travel a lot on river ice. Then we mush through Rainy Pass in the snowy Alaska Range above treeline and return into a heavily timbered area. Past Ophir and McGrath we race along the Yukon River to Kaltag and into the arctic tundra. From Unalakleet we follow the coastal sea ice to Nome.

"The main thing that gets you during the Iditarod is sleeplessness. To complete 1,000 miles in around 15 days, you can't sleep. You may get four hours shuteye each day if you're lucky during the first week. In the final week, one

MUSHER
JOE REDINGTON SR
& HIS IDITAROD TEAM
equipment by... RECREATIONAL EQUIIPMENT
REI
INC.
SUPPORTER OF THE IDITAROD
1000 Miles by Dog Sled
FORD
ALASKA
78
3141 AT

hour a day. When you're not racing, you're feeding the dogs," Butcher said.

"Sometimes I start to hallucinate. I was once on the trail between Ruby and Salatna Crossing, exhausted. It was nighttime, we were in a snowstorm, my headlamp was no use, and the dogs were uppity to keep going.

"As we were moving I fell asleep in the back of the sled. I dreamed that I was on the sled with five other people. My job was to keep us from tipping to the right. Another person was there to keep us from tipping left. Another person was aboard to stop us. We came to some overflow ice, and the team got away from me. I keep a snub rope trailing behind the sled and grabbed it, yelling *whoa*. I woke up pulling on my headlamp cord while the team trotted down the trail. Fortunately they came back for me."

"Often out of 40 teams, 28 will finish," Redington said. "The whites and Indians place well, but the Eskimos, who are less competitive, place poorly. The record time for the Iditarod was 14 days. It was set by Emmet Peters, an Indian from Ruby. Sue and I have placed in the money, finishing on the average in 15 days."

"You know," Redington said, "I had always heard from scientists at the Yukon's North Arctic Institute that dogs couldn't adapt to high altitudes like people could. Blood goes through four stages between sea level and 20,000 feet as your body adapts to less oxygen. Scientists felt that the dogs couldn't adapt.

"Sue and I set out to prove those scientists wrong. In 1979, after we got back from the Iditarod race, we prepared to take a sled team of seven dogs to the 20,320-foot summit of Denali (Mount McKinley). We had never climbed a hill before, and no one had ever taken dogs that high.

"Sue, me, and photographer Rob Stapleton knew how to survive in cold. Other than that, we didn't know what we were doing. We got Ray Genêt to help us, McKinley's foremost guide. He supplied us with gear and accompanied us part of the way." (In the summer of 1980, Genêt died on the way down from the summit of Mount Everest.)

"Everything on the mountain is mental," Butcher said. "You need optimism and patience to conquer bad weather, altitude sickness, and the fear of avalanches. You move when the mountain and its weather let you, which isn't often. We thought our climb was gonna take us 20 days when we started. We were on Denali 44 days in March and April.

"For 30 days out of the 44 we climbed, we never saw the temperature rise above zero. Often it was minus 44 degrees with 100-mile-an-hour gales that bottomed the wind chill factor. We had to wait for three days straight playing cards with our mittens on, just 3,000 feet from the summit. You'd never know when the winds would hit. It would be calm for five seconds, and then a 60-knot gust would grab the tent, only to die again. The winds might strike again in 10 minutes or 10 hours. We kept double-burner Coleman stoves burning. The dogs kept warm by burrowing themselves into the snow."

"We started out with 800 pounds of dog food, 800 pounds of people food, and a ton of gear loaded on sleds pulled by two teams," Redington said. "Genêt turned us loose and gave us a push in the right direction. He then left to guide another expedition. He didn't join us again until we had reached 16,000 feet, except for some emergency help betwen 12,000 and 13,000 feet. We must have made eight relays up that mountain, racing each other's times."

"McKinley is pretty varied terrain," Butcher said. "We flew in to a glacier at 6,000 feet and climbed along it to 10,300 feet. At 9,000 feet there was this hill. I call it a hill, but to us at the time it was the steepest thing we'd seen in our whole lives. When we stopped we'd have to dig our ice axes in to keep the sleds from sliding back. We were exhausted, except for the dogs. We felt that it couldn't get any worse.

"Well, it did get worse. From 10,300 feet the mountain steepens, and there are hidden crevasses. Fortunately the dogs sensed these crevasses and took us around them. Those dogs were crazy. They practically ran us up that mountain pulling from 50- to 200-pound loads. Normally it takes a climber four hours to gain 1,000 vertical feet. We were covering that distance in 45 minutes. It made us dizzy.

"The dogs consistently traveled faster than any person could. The problem was keeping up. Every 30 steps or so, I'd get winded and step on the brake. Five seconds later this damn dog 'Sunny' would bark, and the team would hit the end of the tug. I was too damned tired even to holler *Whoa,* so we'd climb until I winded again in another 30 steps. We were really moving until we hit dirty weather.

"By the time we reached 14,000 feet, we knew that with seven dogs we had too much power to control with ease. We decided to leave the three most powerful dogs tied to a cable staked in the ice. We knew that the final push to the summit would take us at least five days. A woman from another expedition suffering from pulmonary edema volunteered to take care of them for us while she waited for her own people to return. We pressed on to the top."

"We were lucky to have a clear day on the summit of the North American continent," Redington said. "It was only minus 8 degrees, and there was no wind. Fantastic. We stayed up there with the four dogs for two-and-one-half hours and thoroughly enjoyed it."

"In the meantime, 'Mayberry' had been chewing on the cable and managed to cut through," Butcher said. "Before anyone could stop them, three wild-eyed crazy dogs were literally *running* up the trail after us. The woman timed them with her stop watch. To her amazement they ran from 14,000 to 15,000 feet in 10 minutes! They would have kept going if they hadn't gotten tangled in their harnesses on blue ice.

"We found the dogs on our way down from the top, howling and barking. They had dug a huge burrow among some rocks and snow and were waiting for us.

"Our only problem with the dogs, aside from one who was scared of heights, was coming down. On steep slopes there was the danger of the sleds overtaking the dogs. We had to roughlock the sleds by tying chains on the runners that would dig into the ice and snow. We also tied a piece of metal across the sled bottoms so they'd plow. I'd grab the snub rope behind the sled and would dig my heels into the snow and drag. Even so, at times we were out of control.

"When we got to about 12,000 feet, I decided that I'd take all the dogs down to 10,800 feet with a load of gear. It was our first time on ice, and we were still experimenting. Joe said that the sled brake would work fine so we roughlocked the sled lightly. I hopped on with seven crazy dogs pulling.

"As soon as Joe let go of the sled he knew he had made a mistake. I started going faster and faster and hit racing speed. The dogs loved it. Then the sled started to overtake them.

"We hit a bump and flipped at 30 miles an hour.

Meanwhile I was getting dragged along behind, holding on to the sled. Gear was flying off and hitting me, everything was breaking apart, and the dogs were doing all they could to stay out in front.

"Luckily Genêt had taken off half an hour ahead of us. To me he appeared as this bouncing orange dot. Actually, *I* was the one who was bouncing at the time. Between me and Genêt was a crevasse area. If the dogs hit one, they'd break legs or fall completely in.

"Genêt saw us coming, sized up the problem, and braced himself in the trail with his ice axe. When we reached him, he grabbed between the lead and swing dogs. The rest of the team swerved around, coming to a stop.

"I was pretty bruised, the sled was totaled, but none of the dogs were worse for the wear. We picked up our gear strewn all over Denali and roughlocked the sled really well the rest of the way down."

"We never heard the scientific explanation for the success of our dogs," Redington said. "Still, I think we proved our point!"

Cecilia Piper

BARROW, ALASKA

ROADS IN ALASKA ARE CONSPICUOUS BY THEIR ABSENCE. *Consequently, one in every five Alaskans has a license to fly. Most lakes around Fairbanks and Anchorage anchor floatplanes.*

The mortality rate among bush pilots in Alaska is high. Flying conditions, homemade landing strips, and questionable judgment suggest it will remain so. Most pilots crash at least once in their flying careers. Some don't walk away from the scene.

Cecilia Piper is a non-denominational minister from Addison, Maine. In the middle of her life, she had a dream-vision calling her to Barrow, a remote Inuit village on the North Slope of Alaska. She bought a one-way ticket and, over time, became a flying missionary.

Photo by Abbie Sewall.

"IN THE MIDDLE OF MY LIFE I GOT A CALLING TO GO FROM Maine to the Arctic. A vision appeared to me of an Inuit village with some people standing on a ridge watching an airplane land on shore. That's what appeared to me; that's what I saw.

"At age 45, with no support, I bought a plane ticket and went out to Alaska. From Anchorage, I felt compelled towards Point Barrow at the northern tip of Alaska. That's where I was called. When I arrived, everyone tried to send me back, saying I was crazy and that this was no place for a white. I stayed anyway when I learned that a small Eskimo child had also had a vision. When he saw me he ran back to the pastor of the village saying, 'That's the woman *I* dreamed about who was going to help build our church.'

"I rented a small igloo—a wooden shack with a five-foot ceiling. A stove pipe went up through its sod roof. I suffered. Once I contracted pneumonia by breathing in sub-freezing air. I froze my lungs to the point where I was asphyxiated and couldn't breathe. It took me most of a winter to regain my health. I was sick through 65 cold days of darkness. When I recovered I began to work with the Eskimos, telling them not to drink or swap wives. I stayed there for five years.

"An airplane was soon donated to my work. Before I came to Alaska, I had learned to fly out in Maine. In northern Alaska flying was the only way to get anywhere.

"Now, flying over the North Slope is one of the most

treacherous encounters on the face of the earth. It's cold and intense, dark and stormy. At minus 60 degrees, oil lines freeze, planes stall, and you can lose control.

"One danger is frost fog and whiteout conditions. When the ground has snow on it and the sky is white, you lose depth perspective. You can't tell how close your plane is to the ground or mountains. That's not so good when you're flying through a mountain pass.

"You have no radio, and your compass is useless since near the magnetic North Pole everything is north. You have a non-magnetic gyrocompass which you can set. That's fairly accurate over the first hour of flight, but then it must be reset according to a landmark that you're certain of.

"It used to take me two hours and ten minutes to fly to Wainwright. I'd set my compass and then watch for four rivers to pass over. When I hit the Arctic coast, I could find the village.

"My first solo plane trip in the Arctic got me lost in a whiteout in a mountain pass. The ink was still drying on my pilot's license. I didn't have more than 50 hours of flying time. My plane had a good distance range and considerable speed, but I must have touched the skis to the ground several times along the way. I had no airspeed indicator, and ice was beginning to form against the fuselage which dropped all the instrument dials.

"Several hours later I found Wainwright. The man gassing the plane up said, 'You're the first pilot to come in here in three weeks.'

"My hands were sweaty, my jacket soaking wet, and my knees rubbery. I was standing there hanging onto the wing strut when he asked me if I had just come through the pass from Fairbanks.

"I told him, 'Yes,' and he asked, 'Is it clearing?'

"When I told him that it was still pretty thick, he said I did pretty well. He asked how long I had my license.

"'I just got it.'

"His face went white after that. My getting there in those conditions was a miracle. Even the most experienced pilots with hours of instrument flying experience can get vertigo, drop a wing, and it's all over. It was a miracle.

"Another time I learned of 30 Eskimo people who were on a hunting expedition. They had camped on an ice floe. What they didn't know was that the current had changed and they would soon be heading out to sea towards Siberia.

If they didn't get off in time, their frozen corpses would return to Alaska in two months.

"I set off in a plane with another Eskimo named Dave to warn them. We left about midnight, but the summer sun was still out. We would never have left had we known that there was an ice storm and fog over the water.

"In 10 minutes we were 25 miles out to sea. We fought 40-knot headwinds. Sleet and ice formed a crust over the cockpit windshield. We were flying low over the ice to see the expedition, and I had to open the side window and peer down to keep from hitting the ice. We were lost and felt that we would crash at any moment.

"Ice started to fly off the propeller. We were loading up, losing airspeed, and we started to lose altitude. All of a sudden the ice began to melt. I poked Dave and told him to look. On either side of the plane was fog, but straight ahead was a clear thoroughfare. It was like the parting of the Red Sea. We could see far, and 25 miles at the end of that tunnel was the ice floe with the camp of Eskimos. We headed straight for it.

"Now, when I was first learning to fly in Millinocket, Maine, my instructor was pessimistic. He used to get frustrated with me, give up the lesson, and say, 'Let's go bomb bears in Baxter Park.'

"We'd fly past Mount Katahdin and look for some black bears to throw rocks at (brought along specially for that purpose). Finding some bears eating berries in a clearing, we'd toss the rocks at them. We always missed, but it was fun to see them hear the rocks land, stand on their hind legs, and look all around for their hidden assailant.

"Well, over this ice floe I had this bag of coal with a note attached telling the expedition to leave. From my bear bombing experience I knew how to throw this sack of coal out.

"I said, 'Dave, when I pass over the camp, I'll slow-fly the plane and you throw the coal bag down. Hard. If you don't throw it fast enough, it will carry back, hit our tail, and we could crash.'

"That scared Dave so that he threw it exactly as I said. We saw the message land by the little nest of tents on the ice and circled back, fast. Those men now knew what the score was.

"And back down through the tunnel we went. It was still open; the fog was still parted for us, and I could see right back to the village where we came from. I landed the plane, putting her on full throttle into the wind so she wouldn't flip over. When the Eskimos grabbed the wing struts, I cut engine.

"Now, I was still a green pilot at the time. I didn't know that air was warmer over the water which melted the ice on the windshield. Still, it was humanly impossible to do what we did. It was sheer salvation. Try putting your head in a paper bag and running as hard as you can. Get the impression? Only we were running blind at 120 miles per hour.

"I found out later that the Eskimos left the floe in their boats. They had to leave some of their gear and dogs behind, and several months later, the dogs showed up dead. No person could have survived such an ordeal. We had saved their lives."

John Carlson

TALKEETNA, ALASKA

THE ATHAPASKAN WORD FOR "WHERE THE RIVERS MEET" *is Talkeetna. A quaint town by that name rests at the confluence of the Talkeetna, Susitna, and Chulitna rivers.*

For entertainment in Talkeetna, people come to the river banks to watch salmon spawn and to witness sunsets that cast pink blushes of alpenglow across the Alaska Range.

At an annual Moose Festival, unsuspecting tourists are sold local jewelry called "gold nuggets." The stuff is actually gold-painted moose droppings.

Every morning the café is filled with people drinking coffee and debating the politics of the day, such as proposed land legislation or the validity of income taxes.

There is also talk in Talkeetna's café about the time a handwritten sign—"Hippies use side door"—appeared on the front door of the Fairview Inn. The side door was locked. Some-

one ripped the sign down, and when a new sign was posted on the door, the window was smashed. This went on and several more windows were lost. The contest ended in court when the owners of the Inn had the "hippies" subpoenaed and charged with freeloading and disturbing the peace. The bartender maintained he had a right to refuse service to anyone. The judge ruled in favor of the town's establishment, and the next day a new sign appeared on the door: "Rednecks 1. Hips 0."

"We're all rimwallers here," John Carlson said. He fingered his suspenders and stuffed a pinch of Copenhagen snuff inside his cheek.

In place of a knocker, the door to Carlson's house supports an animal trap. He enters, removing his sneakers but not his hat. Inside are bookcases filled with rifle magazines and a library of books on ballistics. He collects ballistics books and mail order catalogs from companies like L.L. Bean and Sears. When he has to leave home, he does so on a bicycle. He keeps no car.

Carlson was formerly a telephone lineman. When he retired, he wavered between alcoholism and religion. Religion won.

"THE FRONTIER BREEDS NONCONFORMISTS WHO LIVE ON the rim of society. Just as I go into Anchorage from here every 18 months, they go into Talkeetna from the bush. They live isolated lives for years. Out there, time is their own; they can live for the minute. They don't have to do other people's bullshit all the time. When they return to

society, many no longer fit in.

"Because it's so peaceful out in the bush, rimwallers visiting town notice noise that the rest of us no longer hear, like the hum of generators and TV sets, airplane engines, and cars. Many are independent thinkers and read a lot. They're aloof from advertising, TV, newspapers, gossip, and chit-chat. They're not a part of the routine of society. When I lived out in the bush, I became an expert on firearm ballistics. I'm a gun nut and have the largest ballistics library outside of Anchorage. Other rimwallers return learned in other things.

"Rimwallers hate to wait on lines. I myself haven't been into city department stores for years. I do most of my shopping by mail. Here are some catalogs from L.L. Bean, R.E.I. Coop, and Sears. I get my Copenhagen snuff mailed to me, my calendars, gunsmithing gear, tools, and clothes. I don't have a car or insurance. When I go into town I ride my bike.

"Other rimwaller types are more extreme. There's a lot of us who refuse to be pushed around by anybody, including the state and federal governments. I know of one old guy who moved back into town after 20 years in the bush. After a year he tore up his driver's license, he tore up his liquor license, and he refused to pay state and income taxes. He said that they're unconstitutional and that they violate his right to privacy by asking how much he earns. Out in the bush, he told me how you follow a different set of laws. Your own. It's as old as the hills. If you have a dispute with someone, you resolve it yourself, one way or another. Sometimes people disappear in the bush and never return. It's easy to hide a body."

"You know, winters in Alaska work on your nerves.

169

When you're living in a basin and the sun comes up at 10:00 and sets at 2:30, you get the impression that it's going to be dark forever. It drives a lot of people to alcohol. I know. It happened to me.

"Northern areas around the world have a problem with alcoholism, from Alaska to Siberia and Sweden. It's terrible.

"I remember when I retired from working on the railroad. I went out and got drunk every night. In the mornings I poured myself a glass of booze and went outside, knowing that the first couple of tries it wasn't gonna stay down. Eventually I developed an ability to control those muscles that swallow and those in the stomach; I could hold the stuff down no matter how saturated I got.

"You think this place looks bad now. It was this deep in empty food tins. I got to the stage where I walked down streets and didn't know where I was. My mind was going. One morning, as I was shaving, I looked in the mirror and said, 'Carlson, I give you six weeks. If you don't get gravel under your feet by then, turn yourself into the Alaska Psychiatric Institute.'

"Six weeks went by. I was walking down the street, and my mind wasn't even on getting drunk. First thing I knew I was in a bar drinking one beer. Then another. I couldn't quit.

"Well, I finally kicked it. Most guys get dried out at Alcoholics Anonymous. I'm a unique case. I got religion. I wore out two missionaries over two years, but finally I accepted Christ. I decided that maybe God wanted me to be an alcoholic. I said in a prayer, 'If that's what you want then I accept it.' I think I got drunk once after that. For most guys out here, they get drunk and stay that way. It's a fact of life in the bush."

Niilo Koponen

FAIRBANKS, ALASKA

NIILO KOPONEN AND HIS WIFE CAME TO ALASKA TO *homestead. Before their first winter they built a one-room cabin on the Chena Ridge near Fairbanks. To bathe they moved the furniture outside, stoked the woodburning stove with kindling, and opened the draft. The room became a sauna, a carryover from Koponen's Finnish upbringing in Manhattan.*

Other homesteaders on Chena Ridge bartered wood and skills for use of the sauna. As rooms were added to the house, christened by Koponen a "hysterical monument," sharing the sauna became a Fairbanks tradition.

Sunday is "open house." More than 50 regulars and newcomers may arrive with watermelons, apples, coffee cakes, and cold drinks to share. Downstairs, uninhibited men, women, and children of all ages strip naked and hang their clothes on hooks that line the walls. They queue up to enter the small, wood-

*panelled sauna. The pine-scented room can hold a score of
sweaty, smiling people.*

*A young woman biologist chats in the sauna with a bush
pilot. He has a beard and ponytail. She tells about her research
at the University of Alaska on arctic wolverines. He mentions
the time he had to fly his Canadian Beaver out of the Anaktu-
vuk Pass in fog.*

*A lady with nothing on but a bandana dips a ladle into a
bucket of cold water. She anoints herself and the person next to
her before pouring a ladleful on the stove. The water sizzles and
turns to steam.*

*Outside on the porch, a large wooden tub is filled with cold
springwater. A bald man resting inside gazes over a meadow of
hay that sweeps down into a forest of spruce. Rising above the
trees is Mount McKinley, its resplendent robes of snow glowing
in the pale moonlight.*

*Refreshments are served throughout the evening. People read
poetry, play music, and share ideas. Koponen wanders in around
nine o'clock. His clothes are covered with straw, his boots with
manure. He's been out working with the horses and disappears
down the stairs to use the sauna.*

*Since coming to Fairbanks Koponen has worked as a miner,
anthropology professor, school principal, political campaigner,
Head Start teacher, and electrician. He is a jack-of-all-trades
by necessity, like others who came to Fairbanks before the oil
pipeline changed the town.*

"I WAS BORN IN 1928 IN NEW YORK CITY TO PARENTS of Finnish descent. I grew up in a Finnish cooperative in a Jewish neighborhood in the Bronx. I spoke Finnish and Yiddish. I remember that we used to have dances, a bowling alley, and a pool hall in Finn Hall located in Harlem. My mother used to act in plays there. Most of these plays had to do with going back to the old country, or were about life in rural settings. I suspect that influenced me, along with the books of Jack London, toward leaving someday to come to Alaska and homestead. A lot of Finns felt the same way and were moving to farms in Maine and Massachusetts, building farmhouses and saunas, and raising families there.

"As I grew up, I became a pacifist like my father and his father. During World War II and later in the Korean War, I was a conscientious objector. I left America for Finland and didn't return until 1948. Then when the Cold War started up, and the McCarthy years, I got a little fed up with politics. I wanted an agrarian lifestyle, but didn't want to leave America. Alaska was a territory at the time, and was in the process of becoming a state. It was also far enough removed from the political scene, and seemed like a decent place to raise a family and live an agrarian lifestyle. So I convinced my wife, Joan, to come with me, and together we applied for 160 acres and a mule under the original 1862 Homestead Act.

"In the territorial days, all the land was public. It was owned by the Feds. And there was a different land ethic.

People didn't claim land for themselves and there weren't 'No Trespassing' signs all over the place. There was little feeling, even on the part of the mining operations, of possessiveness. There was more a collective spirit.

"That public land ethic, in fact, was what stalled the Native Land Claims Settlement Act for awhile. The Indians rightfully felt queasy about giving up what was once all theirs and everyone else's. By accepting part-ownership of the land, they were agreeing to accept a portion of what they once had which amounted to part-ownership of everything. The oil companies bought them out in order to get the pipeline moving. And they did it in very subtle, manipulative ways during the Nixon Administration by forming native corporations. This divided the natives through greed, pitting a new class of native business leaders against the will of the rest of the native people. These business leaders became hustlers and sold out the Indian people and their aboriginal rights to all the land. It was part of the scheme of the vested oil interests to exploit the land. Now, in Alaska, there is a private land ethic—everything is privately owned, including public land.

"Look at federal ownership from the Parks Commission to Fish and Game and the military. The Feds still own tremendous tracts of 'public' land. These federal agencies are no different than corporations unto themselves. They are, in the economic sphere, like bishoprics in the Catholic Church, like principalities in the Holy Roman Empire—entities unto themselves, autonomous and accountable to no one, in practice if not in theory.

"The Army and Air Force still own huge amounts of land. The entire Tanana Valley here is about the size of all of New England minus Maine. One of the Eielson's bombing ranges alone is the size of Massachusetts and Connecticut. And there is a NIKE missile range that goes north from Moose Creek across the Yukon River 70 miles in a huge fan. NIKE missiles have been discontinued now for over 10 years when all the sites were decommissioned. But the missile range itself is still fenced off by an enormous wire mesh fence and 'No Trespassing' signs. It's still 'owned' by the Feds—but the public has long since lost all access and use of that land. Land is power, and the Feds are hanging on to a lot of it, *de facto.*

"Remember there's all this land, but it was hard to get any of it during the last years of the Homesteading Act in the 1970s. When the oil companies moved into Alaska, they wanted the land. And so did the mining companies. And a lot of other politically powerful special interest groups with more clout than you or I. They had no trouble under the D-2 land legislation (which was a section of the Native Land Claims Act) in getting land. Yet that land was never intended for use by private corporations—it was for the people, the public. D-2 and the oil situation politicized the land ethic, and there was a lot of wheeling and dealing.

"A lot of Alaska today is owned by outside interests. In a way it's still territorial and colonial. There is an imperial spirit from the federal and big business agencies. Some companies like the Uranium Corporation of Germany bought up large tracts of land surveyed by the U.S. Geological Survey and said to have mining potential. They just sat on this land for years. Staked it up, along with the big oil companies. Bearcreek Company sounds quaint and grass roots enough. They bought up a lot of land too. Found out they're the exploration subsidiary of Kennecott Mining Corporation.

"In the 1950s when I first came to Alaska with Joan,

there was the *'Mother Earth'* movement being recapitulated in Alaska. People were coming into the country, like me, for the same reasons—to start a new life. Fishers, loggers, miners, and homesteaders who wanted to live close to the land and simply. To escape society. I used to have a teacher who called Alaska the 'Land of the Dropout,' meaning dropouts from society. A lot of us came here.

"A lot of that collective spirit changed when the oil crunch hit. Then a lot of more conservative types came into the area seeking to turn the place into a mirror image of where they came from.

"There was a lot of true frontier pioneer individualism among Alaskans. And then there grew up a lot of pseudo-individualism. Too many people coming in here in their Winnebagos with all their possessions, rather than carrying everything in on a wheelbarrow. These were the guys who lived a vicarious 'pioneer' lifestyle. These weren't the anarchistic sort of old-timers who really carved a life out of a tough land. They were people who lived in ranch houses with one dog on a quarter of an acre. They couldn't find their way out of a closet, but became very vehement in their individualism.

"The pressure to conform to your own brand of individualism is a sign of panic. These people would get all bent out of shape if someone wanted to be an individualist—apart from their own idea of life. They pitched their own mental image of life in Alaska, and it was Big Brother all over again. They were threatened by non-conformism—despite their bumpers being held together by stickers.

"And then there were the guys who thought this was Tombstone, Arizona. It never was the Wild West here, but they pitched that mental image and started carrying gun racks in their pickup trucks. We never used to do that. I knew a guy who came in here and worked with us on telephone line crews. He wore a six-shooter. It used to fall off when he climbed the poles, and we razzed him about it. He got all huffy. He must have watched too many midnight movies on TV.

"Alaska and Fairbanks have changed since I moved here in the 1950s. Back then Fairbanks was about 3,000 people, a small dusty pioneer town. It had one paved street, Cushman. And it was only paved between First and Second, a short block, and between Second and Lacy. It was a dusty, workingman's town.

"People used to say that Fairbanks stored its telephone pole holes in its streets. Moved them around occasionally. I recall my mother coming here to visit. She had no trouble along the entire unpaved Alcan Highway. Turned off Cushman onto First and broke her oil pan.

"People used to say that Fairbanks was the only place

where you could stand in ice and water up to your neck and have dust blow in your face. It was like something out of the '30s until Alyeska moved in—an army of occupation in yellow pickup trucks, here to build a pipeline. The oil pipeline was run by ex-sergeants who joined Bechtel. Fairbanks was like Vietnam, only we were on the receiving end. I understand now how the people felt when the Mongol hordes descended on the land.

"Today you fly over the town and instead of a sleepy, walkable town, you see a big, spread-out parking lot. Took us a little longer than Anchorage, but we, too, got developed and Los Angelized.

"Anyway, I came here to homestead. A friend of mine from Wyoming once said that homesteading was Uncle Sam's original answer to agricultural overproduction. People were given all this scrub land to work and cultivate. It wasn't very productive until years later.

"I was lucky. I managed to get my 160 acres. Selected a site oriented south in the sun so it wasn't subject to much permafrost and we could get solar heat. I like the university area here on the Chena Ridge. Got in before all the land was closed off completely after the 1970 Native Land Claims Settlement Act.

"Under the Homesteading Act, you had to build a house and prove that you lived in it for five years, at least seven months a year. You had to clear and cultivate a quarter section, 20 acres. You had to do these things unless you were a veteran or a GI, which I wasn't. The land office overlooked inspections for veterans, and they got land first.

"We started out here building a movable wanigan which I winched up the hill on skids with my old Dodge. A friend of mine was a stone mason who got his tombstones shipped in crates. He saved up all the two-by-fours, and with that wood we erected the little room around the sauna here. At the time we slept in a loft over the sauna, to keep warm. We gradually added on to it, dubbing the place with a small plaque a 'hysterical monument.' Those railroad ties are meant to be temporary. Someday I'll get around to replacing them. We also built the barn and cleared a 15-acre pasture, a 12-acre field, and my neighbor's 20-acre field. We helped raise a neighbor's 28 goats, in addition to our own family.

"To make ends meet, I took various jobs like teaching, which gave me my summers and those long sunny nights to work on the place.

"Our open sauna started by necessity. At the time, there were few places in Fairbanks to take a bath. So our neighbors would haul water and wood here and use the sauna. They invited their friends. And soon it spread, over 25 years, to an 'open house' sauna on Sunday nights.

"I like living here. My lifestyle is now a nice balance of physical and intellectual labor. For a while I was interested in a small self-generating community. It didn't develop since living in Alaska is like living in a revolving door—people are always coming and going. It's hard to establish any continuity in a group and, at the same time, I'm not into a bureaucratic society. It has to be open to consensus, evolution, and change.

"Alaska has changed, but there's still a little of that frontier spirit left. You can see it here in the Interior, especially when it gets to minus 70 degrees outside and people are walking around breathing in ice crystals. The cold kind of sets this place apart. There's still plenty of spirit left in the place."

180

Larry Katkin

FAIRBANKS, ALASKA

WINTER IN THE INTERIOR OF ALASKA BRINGS WITH IT A *chilled beauty. At minus 80 degrees, a profound stillness hangs in the air. Breath crystallizes. Trees crackle. In the long nights stars glitter coldly against a pulsating Aurora that flares and fades with green and red streamers.*

Far north in the Brooks Range there is perfect isolation except for one 48-inch-wide intrusion—the Alaska oil pipeline. It runs for 800 miles from Prudhoe Bay to holding tanks in the port of Valdez. From there it's shipped to refineries in the South 48. Eventually the oil returns to Alaska where it is stored in the holds of local gas stations.

Larry Katkin worked on the trans-Alaska pipeline as a frozen-soils engineer. When the project was completed, he remained in Fairbanks and opened a gas station and a lock-smithing business.

182

Katkin tells how the pipeline was an entire lifestyle that changed Fairbanks and its culture overnight. The pipeline, for Katkin, represented the American dream — and the American nightmare.

"I'M FROM PENNSYLVANIA AND WAS BORN IN 1949. I came to Alaska at age 20 for two reasons. Reason number one is that this is the furthest point on the North American continent I can go to get away from my Jewish mother. No way would she fly, and it's too far to drive. Reason number two is that I always wanted to be a geologist. I came to Fairbanks to study geology at the University of Alaska.

"One thing I learned—Alaska is a land of dreams! Everybody gets their dreams fulfilled here if they work at it and if they wait long enough. I used to read earth science books when I was a kid. I said, 'Wow, Man, that's what I want to be when I grow up.' Twenty-three years later, when I was out on the North Slope working on a drilling pad for the Alaska oil pipeline in minus 45 degrees, and there were miserable whiteout conditions and creeping frostbite, I stopped and paused in the middle of my work and thought: 'Gee, I did it. I'm a geologist.' From that time on, all my dreams out here just kept on coming through.

"Another dream was the house we're sitting in. I built it myself. When I was in college, we were a lot of hippies. We used to hold our parties out here on the Chena Ridge just outside town. I looked around and said that someday I'd like

to own a place just like this. Soon afterwards, the whole place burned down. The parties were pretty fantastic, you see.

"Well, there came a time soon after getting out of college when I had to start applying for jobs. I knew a lot about frozen soils from geology class. R&M Geological Consultants was hired by the Alyeska Corporation, a consortium of oil companies which contracted out to have the oil pipeline built. R&M's job was to analyze the soil for 800 miles from the port of Valdez to Prudhoe Bay. R&M needed a quality control inspector who knew a lot about frozen soils, a specialty field.

"Well, this manager was on the phone when I walked into his office. He was yapping about how frozen soils people were hard to come by. On his desk he had three jars filled with soil from the area. He asked me to define the silt, gravel, and sand in the jars by weight, not by volume. I knew how to do this, and took a kind of guess. I was right on, and soon found myself in charge of a $130 million dam project. I was still a hippie with long hair and everything, you know.

"When I got the job with R&M, I started to look for a place to live. I went to the real estate agent in Fairbanks and in a photo recognized a burned-out house as the one where these great college parties were held. Five acres were going for just $1,000 an acre. I bought it, built this house, and moved in. It's now commercially zoned and worth 10 times that amount. Alaska—land of dreams.

"Just recently I decided to go into business for myself. I looked around and said, 'Gaz-o-line. Try gaz-o-line.' At the time, some Caterpillar D-9 bulldozers were pushing dirt around, grading the road in front of my house. I ambled over to one of the Cat drivers and said, 'Hey, could you push a little of that dirt over here?' They said they could. And, for a few bucks on the side, they did. I soon had myself a graded driveway. Normally, Cats rent for more than $90 an hour.

"Then I called up Texaco and asked if they had any used pumps. I was interested in selling gaz-o-line. They said they did. I gave them $900 dollars, got my two pumps, hooked them up, and then called again.

" 'Could you drop off 6,000 gallons of gaz-o-line?'

"They could. At the time, the price of gas was high. I decided to undercut every other gas station around by some humungous amount. I earned only three cents profit on every gallon. But people pulled in to buy *my* gas. I was selling 4,000 gallons of gas a day from the day I opened. Gas was around 69 cents a gallon, and I was making more than $100 a day profit. It pissed off the other gas station owners, and soon Texaco tightened up on gas quotas. But by that time, I sold out the business and went into locksmithing. Alaska—land of dreams.

"Let me tell you about the Alaska pipeline. Back in the 1960s when things were just getting started, I was in college. The pipeline started out as some abstract concept. What did it mean? The consciousness of the pipeline hadn't really sunk in yet.

"You see, you don't know what a pipeline of this magnitude is until it *happens* to you. Here was the biggest construction project in the world, built by Bechtel—the largest construction company in the world—running through Fairbanks—one of the smallest towns in the world. Bechtel builds other projects such as nuclear power plants for Westinghouse, dams, and Saudi pipelines. Big.

"Not really knowing what the pipeline was, we sort of

knew that we were against it. Fairbanks in the 1960s was a way of life as well as a town. There were the conservatives and the hippies. But despite your politics, everybody pitched in and helped everyone else. If there was a car accident, everybody stopped to help out, pull the car out of the culvert with a jeep and cable, share around some beers, jive each other. No cost. Just altruistic help.

"Sure enough, after the pipeline moved in, things changed. The pipeline doesn't just go through a town, it encompasses it. It changed the whole economy of the town. And it changed the character of the people. Now, people are too busy, and the town is too bustling. People today don't have time for each other. When I needed help on my house here, my friends were charging pipeline wages. The whole spirit of this place changed.

"Some of us held out for a while; we weren't going to go to the labor halls and hire ourselves out to work on the pipeline. This was after 1969 when they had completed their billion dollar study of where the thing would go. It was interesting to see people hold out for a year or two, and then sell out. Everybody had a price. I did. You begin to rationalize. America needs this oil and this pipeline. They're going to build it whether I work on it or not. So why shouldn't I be making $7,000 a month in labor wages?

"I was hired as a soils engineer. For each soil type, there was a different construction mode. Depending on the soil, you built the pipeline above or below the ground. First they built a work pad, which was an 800-mile road that would lead along the pipe. Prior to the work pad, there were no roads. They built the 800-mile Haul Road. They put in the pipeline—all above the permafrost on the delicate tundra. The road was slate. Tundra is hard to drive on—you sink in.

"They insulated the road and work pad with 800 miles of blue styrofoam. It's expensive—maybe $10 a sheet then. The whole scene was incredible. Bechtel was literally an army. They took over the army base in Fairbanks. It involved the logistics of running an army 30,000 strong.

"What started out as a projected $9-million project ended up costing more than $9 billion when construction was finally completed around 1977. Alyeska was terribly mismanaged and there was terrible waste, but the end result was a very good, well-built pipeline.

"So I got into it. In Fairbanks, things were literally changing by the minute. I was once involved with looking at Alyeska's purchase orders. They were piled three feet high on a desk in some bureaucrat's office. The first purchase order was for 3,000 yellow pickup trucks. The second was for 3,000 more. Just pickup trucks.

"Well, these things started coming in on the railroad, yellow truck after yellow truck. Here's this small town with no yellow pickup trucks. The next day there's nothing *but* yellow pickup trucks. I mean, we didn't know what to do with all of 'em. So we gave one to every engineer and to every secretary. You could have three if you wanted.

"Not only did parts and supplies and yellow pickup trucks start arriving in Fairbanks, but people as well. We had people from all over the South 48 coming here to work on the pipeline. There was a love-hate relationship between Alaskans and Texans. These guys in cowboy hats kept on arriving at the airport. On one billboard in town, I remember the slogan: 'Happiness is a Texan running home with an Okie under each arm.' There was a lot of resentment as the town started to change.

"When news of pipeline wages spread, the labor halls

started to fill up. How many chances in a lifetime can you make $6,000 a month for labor work?

"What would happen is that Alaskan residents were theoretically given first preference for pipeline jobs. Alaskan natives were guaranteed jobs. You'd go to the labor hall and be assigned to different pump stations along the Haul Road. They might have 100 jobs and call out ticket holders 1 through 100. That was your A list. It was the good jobs. In one day, maybe 400 jobs might come through. The labor halls were like an army dispatch center.

"As the jobs were filled, good jobs were harder to come by. There were soon three lists: A, B, and C. The C list was the shitty jobs that no one wanted, like cleaning latrines. After so many hours of work, you got moved into the B list, and then to the A list. That's how the union worked at the time.

"Then things started to get weird. People started to buy their way in. I remember how one day, everyone is Alaskan and speaks English in the labor hall. The next day, everyone is speaking Irish. And they're getting jobs! What happened was the Irish Republican Army was bribing the dispatchers. I.R.A. workers could keep a part of their wages and send the rest of their money home to finance their war in Belfast! The next day, everyone might be speaking Spanish and hail from Argentina. They got in on the minority hire system. Women, then, were also minorities.

"Other people came in to feed off the pipeline economy. People like shopkeepers, shopping center boomers, and bar proprietors. And prostitutes. Fairbanks was changing by the moment.

"I remember how the biggest thrill in town was to drive down and watch the prostitutes. In the early 1970s I didn't even know what they looked like. A friend of mine pointed them out—they walked a little sexier and seemed to go nowhere in front of the bars on Second Avenue, which was called by the cowboys in town, 'Two Street.'

"All of a sudden, the whole street was a show. I sat down on the hood of my car and just watched. One night a negro minister was sitting on the sidewalk with his entire congregation, singing hymns and preaching. He saw a black prostitute go by and yelled out to her, 'Sister, you can't be a whore all your life!' The congregation answered 'Amen!' in response. It was hysterical. Except for the natives.

"The native culture was very beautiful. Past tense. It's going very quickly. The United States government worked very subtly to bring the natives back into our society in return for getting the Alaska pipeline moving in the 1970s. By giving the natives land compensation, they traded away their aboriginal rights to that land. Indians had to abide by the government's rules and regulations. By guaranteeing natives jobs on the pipeline project, the government took people from a barter-subsistence economy and brought them back into a cash economy. The natives could no longer hunt, trap, fish, and build their own houses for a living.

"What white society did was to create a dependency. The natives were outside the System. The System tells you to go to school, get married, get a job, and contribute taxes to social security and the Gross National Product. You're sup-posed to enjoy yourself in between work. That's the way you and I were brought up.

"That was not life for the natives. As long as they weren't part of the System, they were free to enjoy them-selves. Cash economy is a subtle form of slavery. It leads one to a credit economy. As soon as you are a cog in the machine,

you have to work for a living. To get a job you have to live in town and buy food at the grocery store. You buy your clothes from commercial retailers. You pay cash or rely on credit. You begin to forget how to make your own clothes. You need a permit to hunt game that once supplied you with hides.

"At some point along the line you're not working because you *want* to work, but because you *have* to work. If you stop working, you lose everything. Then you're forced on welfare. You're a slave of the System. That's the American way. That's the degradation of native culture.

"It doesn't end there for the natives. When the pipeline was completed, and their land was gone, they were up against the old discriminations. Now most natives are unemployed and on welfare. They are poorly educated. They've lost control of their lives.

"To understand how the pipeline could destroy both the Fairbanks and native cultures, you have to understand the mentality of the people who organized the project. Apart from war, the Alaska pipeline was perhaps the greatest concentration of waste and mismanagement in the world. This, in part, was because of greed—America needed the oil. Soon afterwards we were faced with a real, or engineered, oil shortage that drove this entire nation into controlled chaos. There was plenty of politics involved, believe me. Part of that shortage was artificial; it was a ploy to get the pipeline moving and the native claim to aboriginal land and rights settled. The natives sold out, and Alyeska moved in.

"You have to remember that the pipeline was a cost-plus project backed by U.S. government guaranteed loans. Cost-plus here meant that the government gave Alyeska 10 percent on top of what it cost to get the pipeline built. If the pipeline cost $1,000 to build, Alyeska made a $100 profit. If the pipeline cost $9 billion to build, 10 percent of that was a hefty profit. So there was plenty of institutionalized waste. The more laborers spent, the more profit Alyeska made. This led to waste and mismanagement. And the oil companies didn't care. They made windfall profits on the oil in the years that followed.

"The waste was incredible. Laborers were fed steak, lobster — anything — in addition to huge wages. I saw guys feeding steak to the bears, just to see bears up close. When the work pad was being built, there was plenty of wood that was cut down. Rather than shipping it down to Fairbanks on the hundreds of empty trucks that returned to town, they burned it. The way they burned it was to take a diesel truck used to fuel the Cat bulldozers. I watched one guy spray 300 gallons of diesel fuel on a pile of wood. It took him 10 minutes. He drove the truck away and set a torch to the pyre. I guess it was fun to watch the huge billow of flame and black smoke that followed. But he could have started the whole thing with a five-cent match.

"There was a lot of corruption. I heard of one guy that took a D-9 Cat out on to the tundra when no one was looking. It's an expensive piece of machinery. He bulldozed a big hole and then drove in. He covered the Cat up and returned after the pipeline was built to dig out the bulldozer and sell it.

"Another form of corruption was to tell the government that a D-9 Cat was broken, and request every single part be replaced, using the one serial number. You could make more than $500,000 that way.

"At one point I got cabin fever. I had been sitting in this office for what seemed like all winter. I had nothing to do. I was going nuts. I told my foreman to make up some excuse — anything to get me out of the office for a while.

"I was sent north of the Yukon River to set up labs at the camps along the Haul Road. I thanked my foreman and went home for five days. No one knew, or cared, where I was.

"After that, I flew up to the first camp. The labs were all set up, but I discovered that everybody needed things from town. So I got a hold of a truck and made a big list. I filled the truck on the next trip with everything from sneakers to pot, magazines, and booze. Because I was an engineer, I got the guy who went with me to do the lifting. It was all hush hush since only the Teamsters were supposed to be driving trucks on the road. I stored all my goodies in soil testing crates.

"Well, when people saw us they were delighted. They took care of us. They even offered to put us up in the girls' dorms. Anything. The best rooms, food, even a special showing of 'Deep Throat.'

"One day we had a huge blizzard on the Slope. It was minus 50 degrees and there was zero visibility. I was in the truck with my partner. We were going two miles an hour. He had to get out and walk in front of the truck, looking for the road. He almost got frostbitten, but we made it to Franklin Bluffs, our base camp.

"At Franklin Bluffs camp, I told the guys that I was sent there to inspect the food. We got real good food! They put us in the room reserved for the president of Alyeska. He never visited the place anyway. But even that got boring. We were cabinbound and the storm raged on.

"One night, I'm sitting on the bed in the suite and I say to my partner, 'Hey, let's go to Fairbanks!'

"It's more than 300 miles south of the camp but he's